QUANTUM SELF HYPNOSIS
Awaken the Genius Within

Jo Ana Starr, PhD

© Jo Ana Starr 2011 all rights reserved. No part of this book may be reproduced or transmitted by any means without the express written permission of the author.

ISBN-13:- 978-1468007633

ISBN-10: 1468007637

TABLE OF CONTENTS

Chapter 1 Introduction to Self Hypnosis……..…..…...…..5

Chapter 2 The Magic in Your Mind ………...........…......15

Chapter 3 History of Hypnosis….........….................………25

Chapter 4 Hypnotic Influences….........….................………31

Chapter 5 Self Hypnosis Explained................................55

Chapter 6 How Self Hypnosis Works..............…………...65

Chapter 7 Master Self Hypnosis Inductions..…...…......77

Chapter 8 Self Hypnosis Session Scripts…....................113

Chapter 9 Writing Your Own Self Hypnosis Scripts....217

Chapter 10 Setting the Stage for Success…...…............225

Chapter 11 Adjusting to the New You...…....................235

Chapter 12 Assuring Your Success……......................241

Disclaimer and Terms of Use: The Author and Publisher has striven to be as accurate and complete as possible in the creation of this book, notwithstanding the fact that she does not warrant or represent at any time that the contents within are complete due to the rapidly changing nature of the world. While all attempts have been made to verify information provided in this publication ,the Author and Publisher assumes no responsibility for errors, omissions, or contrary interpretation of the subject matter herein. Any perceived slights of specific persons, peoples, or organizations are unintentional. In practical advice books, like anything else in life, there are no guarantees of outcomes. Readers are cautioned to rely on their own judgment about their individual circumstances and to act accordingly. This book is not intended for use as a source of medical or counseling advice. All readers are advised to seek the services of competent professionals in the medical or mental health fields, as deemed necessary.

CHAPTER 1
INTRODUCTION

A Certified Clinical Hypnotherapist and Director of the New England Institute of Hypnotherapy, Dr. Jo Ana Starr, PhD trained in 1987 with the American Institute of Hypnotherapy under the tutelage of the esteemed Dr. Krasner. She later earned a PhD and holds a Doctorate in Divinity as well. Her undergraduate work is in English and Psychology. Dr. Starr has made numerous appearances on both radio and television programs to discuss topics such as Hypnosis and Wellness. She is in the process of completing 3 other books on related topics, and has authored 8 training programs, all focused on Hypnosis, Prosperity, and Wellness.

Like many people, you've probably heard that Self Hypnosis has helped millions of people achieve their goals. You were likely skeptical, with images of stage hypnotists making volunteers look positively silly up there on the stage. In spite of that, you may have considered investigating

Hypnosis more thoroughly to see if it could help you with a few issues of your own. In fact, that is probably the reason you bought this book. You hope to learn more about Hypnosis and to see whether it's a good fit for you. Good for you! I think you're on the right track!

The reasons that you and others find their way to Hypnosis or Self Hypnosis are as different as we humans are. Maybe you'd like to lose weight, or just lose your love of donuts. Maybe you want to learn to stay motivated and working at your current priorities, or to stop smoking once and for all. For some folks, work or business related challenges bring them to Hypnosis. Hypnosis used for sales success, for example, is a great application and one that has helped thousands of sales people improve their sales numbers.

Or maybe you're feeling stressed out with the economic woes in our country and in the world. Maybe you'd like to find a way to let go of your worries and to find positive outlets for your concerns, getting free of stress and anxiety. Accomplishing these ideal outcomes with Self Hypnosis is entirely doable; in fact, it's also pleasant and easy.

The ideal applications for Self Hypnosis are almost limitless. Some individuals live under the dark cloud of mental confusion; whether hormonal or chemical, working with less than full brain power makes all their tasks harder than they should be. How much would your life improve if you could quickly, pleasantly and easily gain focus and pinpoint concentration? Would you like to lose those "senior moments" that I've even heard 30 year olds complaining about? Most of us have some aspect of our lives and our belief systems that could use a bit of upgrading. Self Hypnosis is the fastest, least expensive and easiest way to give your life a facelift.

Many individuals want to experience Hypnosis but hesitate to go to a stranger for help. And the image of the poor stage hypnosis subjects being made to feel silly doesn't help at all, either, does it? It can be hard to walk into someone's office and share information that may be personal and sensitive. And frankly, there are good Hypnotherapists and the opposite out there too, so how do you know which one you will find?

There are probably as many valid reasons not to go to a professional Hypnotherapist as there are reasons *to* go to one. Some of the reasons that keep individuals from taking the plunge and seeing a Certified Hypnotherapist are these:

Time - It can take hours with drive time.
Cost - It can be really expensive.
Trust issues - It can be tough to opening up to a stranger.
Performance anxiety – Can this work?
Fear - Change can be scary.

It's a shame that these concerns and others keep a lot of individuals from experiencing the healing power of Hypnosis.

Well, I have great news for you! The purpose of this book is to help you to become a Self Hypnosis Master, able to access all the genius abilities hidden in your mind and put that genius to work, helping you to get free of any barriers that may be blocking the way to your highest good.

Imagine having all the tools and training in your own hands to create the changes in your life that you want in a timely, cost-effective way. With someone you trust, with all the time in the world to work with hypnosis until you are entirely comfortable with the process. Quantum Self Hypnosis takes you by the hand and shows you how to use Hypnosis to massively improve the quality of your life easily, pleasantly and effectively!

This book provides you with 5+ Master Self Hypnosis Inductions, including Quick inductions, Classic inductions and a new percussion-based induction as well as 20 full length professional behavior and belief modification Self Hypnosis session scripts. These are not shortcut inductions. These are full inductions that will take you as little as 20 minutes all the way up to 45 minutes depending on your needs. Even more importantly, you will learn how to create your own custom behavior modification sessions for topics not covered in the provided Self Hypnosis session scripts. You will learn how to create powerful sessions for any application you can imagine.

Please do not confuse Quantum Self Hypnosis with other books or audio programs about Hypnosis or Self Hypnosis. This book is a condensed version of an 18 hour professional Hypnosis Certification training program that has been fine-tuned into a nuts and bolts book for laymen, designed to turn each and every reader into Self Hypnosis Masters. There are no gimmicks here - no Immediate Hypnosis or Underground Hypnosis or any of the other forms of Hypnosis or sort-of Hypnosis that are being marketed online.

This is a bottom line book that gives you insider's access to the training material taken directly from a $300.professional Hypnosis certification program!! And don't think it's going to be too complex for you. It's not; all of the training information is designed to help newcomers create effective Self Hypnosis sessions that will change their lives! As this is not the usual Self Hypnosis book that tells you all about

Hypnosis without actually teaching you how to use it, *Quantum Self Hypnosis* fully prepares you to use Self Hypnosis the way that trained professionals use it. This book is complete and it includes everything you will need to succeed, other than a comfortable chair, some time, a quiet spot and an audio file or CD.

As if that were not enough, to assure that you have quick success with your Quantum Self Hypnosis project, we have created a FREE members website. There are several great reasons you might want to do that. First of all, the member website will include a forum for members, occasional email updates for members only, but mostly to get the FREE $59 Audio Self Hypnosis session created by Dr. Starr. Using this session is a great Hypnotic pre-conditioner to your own sessions by getting your mind accustomed to experiencing Hypnosis and totally immersing yourself in the natural cadence of Hypnosis. This Quantum Self Hypnosis session suggests that you easily grasp the material taught in the book, that you feel comfortable using Self Hypnosis, and that your success is assured.

If you've already read a lot of books on Self Hypnosis, this is probably the one you've been waiting for. Easy to read and easy to implement, this revolutionary book offers you many of the same benefits that trained professional Hypnotists enjoy. You are getting insider access to training material that has proven itself over the last 16 years. Your success *is* assured!

You are clearly someone who wants to find effective tools for positive personal change or perhaps someone is considering the possibility of beginning a career as a Hypnotist or Hypnotherapist, or maybe you just want to help friends and family. We congratulate you on your choice of what we believe to be the most powerful, pleasant, effective and easy to use self-help tool - Self Hypnosis. It's exciting to think of all the wonderful changes you will create in your life.

In terms of value to you, we want this book or e-book to be the best money you have spent on a self-help book. We have worked hard to make it as good as it can be and we'd like feedback from you. Whether you purchased your book or e-book on Amazon or elsewhere, please consider taking a moment to leave feedback at Amazon to help others decide whether this book is a good choice for them.

I have spent the last 16 years training individuals as Certified Clinical Hypnotherapists and Certified Hypnotists. We at NEIH.COM take great pride in the successes of our graduates and we want your experience to be a successful one as well. If we can help you, please feel free to call our office or email us. You can find our contact information at http://neih.com. Thanks in advance for buying this book and we sincerely hope you enjoy it!

CHAPTER 2
THE MAGIC IN YOUR MIND

If you are reading this page, you have just made one of the best decisions of your life! Taking a chance by trying something new is a way of declaring loudly to the Universe "I trust that I can accomplish whatever I set my mind to." This is one of the most ratifying viewpoints a human can have. Making a commitment and trusting that you can succeed moves you closer to your goal.

Don't worry; there's no cliff-diving here, but any new action or commitment holds within it the possibility of great success or the opposite. With our guidance, we are confident that each of you is poised at the edge of revealing and using your Inner Genius to create magic in your life.

I'm excited for you; you have a great inner journey ahead that can bring you peace and happiness and whatever else you desire. I can only imagine how dreary my life might have been if I had not dug and dug until I found the information that changed my life and that's going to change yours.

Oh, and by the way, welcome to the 10% Club! Statistics show that 10% or fewer of the population actively uses their minds to create value for themselves and others. Whether you are using that much brain juice right at this exact moment doesn't matter. You will be soon and that's what counts.

We will go into the mechanics of Self Hypnosis later but right now let's define Hypnosis a bit. First of all, Hypnosis is an induced state of relaxation in which expectation and belief play a part. Being in a hypnotic state looks and sometimes feels like being asleep although in the beginning it feels more like being a bit zoned with someone talking to you very slowly in the background. In the case of Self Hypnosis, that someone is you. Self Hypnosis is the process of your working with yourself using an audio recording or audio file that allows you to act as both the client and the

Hypnotist. So you're probably wondering how you can be talking to yourself and in a deeply relaxed state at the same time, and the answer is you can't. You can, however, record a "session" and replay it on your computer or an mp3 player. Now again, don't get nervous. You will learn all the ins and outs of this process as we go along, so relax.

Let's get back to defining Hypnosis. Hypnosis is a high-learning state in which the subject is induced into a deep state of relaxation, allowing him to move beneath the conscious mind and to awaken the subconscious mind. The subconscious mind is the creative, subjective part of the brain that responds to symbols, color, sounds, smells, and light. The subconscious mind is child-like, open and receptive to new ideas and thoughts. This is the part of your brain that allows you to create poetry, take great photos, draw, paint, and imagine, etc. The subconscious mind is usually associated with the right hemisphere of the brain or the right brain and the conscious mind is usually associated with the left hemisphere of the brain, or the left brain. The reason we want to move beneath the conscious mind is that in human beings, the conscious mind's job is to maintain homeostasis or keep everything the same. The drive to maintain homeostasis is the opposite of change, as you know. Easy, fast and permanent change requires the Self Hypnotist to access the subconscious mind because this childlike aspect of mind loves change and the creative process. In fact, the subconscious mind is designed for change and learning.

You can think of the conscious mind in terms of the inner adult, logical, objective, engaging in orderly behavior, orderly tasks with full awareness of time and schedules. Your conscious mind is like your inner grownup whereas your subconscious mind is more like your inner child.

You will hear people say, "Jack is really a left-brain kind of guy. He's very orderly, neat, likes statistics, keeps a tidy desk, and seems to value order about all else." As you might imagine, certain careers would appeal to this individual such as working as an attorney, accountant, engineer, bookkeeper, statistician, scientist, researcher, software engineer, soldier and so on.

You will also hear people say, "Sally is so creative, she can make anything by hand but she can't balance her checkbook or remember to get to appointments on time. She's like a kid. She's scatterbrained a lot of the time." We've all known people who are so creative and child-like that functioning in the real world is hard for them. Careers that attract these individuals are naturally art, photography, graphic design, fashion, elementary school teaching, landscaping, architects, builders, and so on.

Ideal brain use would be balanced brain hemisphere function and thus a balanced use of the conscious mind and subconscious mind, but truly balanced mind/brain function is pretty unusual. Most people use one half of the brain most of the time, although most of us access both hemispheres of the brain many times daily.

This information is helpful to you for identifying which of these groups you and friends or family fit into. Right-brain dominant individuals are generally easier to hypnotize; these are the creative types. They are curious about the process and when you use a variety of suggested sounds, smells, colors and light images, they are very easy to engage. Left-brain dominant individuals usually need a bit more time to get into a full state of hypnosis and prefer a bit less imagery. Of the included Master Hypnosis Inductions, some work better with one group than the other and we indicate that information when applicable with each Master Self Hypnosis Induction.

No matter what you've read, I want you to know that everyone who is a hearing individual with an IQ above about 85 can be hypnotized. Unusually intelligent/intellectual people are very easy to hypnotize as long as you give them (or you) a long slow induction; the boredom of it all drops them like a rock. Interestingly, these peoples usually have the belief that they will be difficult to hypnotize.

And if you can't figure out which category you or someone you might work with, fall into, don't worry. Use a long, slow induction and a slower behavior modification suggestion phase and watch for respiratory changes. When you are working with yourself, you're all set. One of the big advantages of Self Hypnosis over Hypnosis is that we all like to hear our own voices playing in our heads; we believe what we're hearing and we usually go easily and deeply into just the right state because we trust ourselves.

In summary, Hypnosis is an induced state that allows the subject to enter a highly-creative, high learning state. Self-Hypnosis is exactly like Hypnosis, except that the individual hypnotizes himself by listening to a self-created CD or audio file.

Here's an important question we are asked all the time. Why go to all the trouble of learning Self Hypnosis when you can buy a CD online at EBay for $9.99? And the answer to that question is both simple and complex.

The simple answer is another question. Why do you eat steak when dog food would probably provide the same nutritional value at a fraction of the cost of steak? Well, I would argue that at least we know what's in the steak; one can only imagine what's in the dog food. Also the steak tastes much better and it's a much more pleasant experience. Ditto your custom Hypnosis session versus the EBay $9 CD. When you produce your own CD or audio file, you have absolute control over the quality of the session. You can make specific suggestions that reinforce the rewards and reasons that motivate you to want to make certain changes. A generic CD is not a perfect fit for you but if it's well-done it's probably better than nothing. Conversely, a self-created Hypnosis session is probably better than anything else, because it's created specifically for you and by the person who cares the most about the quality of your session.

The complex answer is this. Hypnosis works. Whatever the CD suggests will affect you and your life. Since the EBay CD might actually put you into Hypnosis, you will not know exactly what the speaker is saying. You also don't know if that person is well trained or trained at all, and that session most certainly was not custom designed for you. We're dealing with your mind here, arguably the most important part of your body; so this isn't something you want to get wrong. Remember, garbage in, garbage out. And I have to say this also. If your level of commitment to make meaningful change in your life is $9, then we're dealing with a whole new challenge here. A well designed and executed Self Hypnosis session can be so highly effective that its value is beyond question.

Again, you can see that I get kind of excited about all of this because it is important. If you knew that you had a winning lottery ticket and you couldn't find it, would you be upset? That beautiful piece of human real estate sitting up there in your head is more valuable than any lottery ticket because it can create for you everything that the cash from that lottery ticket could, including the cash. And lots more. Get committed to getting to know your brain a lot better and your brain will reward you grandly.

OK, so you now have a bit of an idea of what hypnosis is, also what self-hypnosis is, and why and how they work. We will get much more detailed as we progress through the program, but this has been a good start. The most important piece of information you can take away from this first section is this. You are a person who can create anything you choose to create, largely because you have been gifted with a limitless mind and a generous human spirit.

Fortunately, you can access that limitless mind easily and quickly through the use of Self Hypnosis. Hold that thought in your mind for a moment. Imagine your ideal life sitting squarely in your hand, close your eyes and savor that possibility. As a human being with a limitless mind, you are a genius. You are going to learn throughout this training how to nurture and encourage your inner genius to guide you to your highest outcome.

CHAPTER 3
HISTORY OF HYPNOSIS

I'm not going to spend too much time on this topic because frankly, it's not critically important to your success. I do, however, think it is important to have a bit of context on the origins of Hypnosis, so I'm going to mention the 5 or 6 key figures and give you a bit of background.

MESMER

The Father of Hypnosis, Mesmer, presented a paper called *The Influence of the Stars and Planets as Curative Powers* to the University of Vienna in 1773. Mesmer claimed that the planets affected humans thru an invisible fluid he called Animal Magnetism. He believed that this substance could be derived from a magnet, and that all cellular structures had an affinity for it. He left Vienna and worked in Paris with great success, running Mesmer's Haven, a place where he demonstrated Hypnosis, in an unusual way. After living a life of affluence he lost favor; things went downhill and he returned to Vienna a pauper.

MARQUISE DE PYSEGUR

De Pysegur, a former student of Mesmer, began by hypnotizing peasants for his amusement. He discovered Artificial Somnambulism, which demonstrated the first contention of Hypnosis, which is that a state analogous to sleep can be produced artificially in an entirely awake individual. He believed that while in that state, the thoughts and actions of the client are under the control of the Hypnotist.

FATHER GASSNER

Gassner, a Jesuit priest in Southern Germany, demonstrated Hypnosis in a frightening way by hypnotizing a young peasant girl to death. He succeeded in bringing her back, and in the process, her damaged leg was healed, causing quite a stir. Father Gassner hypnotized many others before and after this event with similar results.

DR. JAMES BRAID

Dr. Braid, an English surgeon, is known as the father of the scientific evaluation of Hypnosis, for challenging the mystical claims of Mesmer and his followers. He was a scientist, and gave us the word Hypnosis, from the Greek word Hypnos. He postulated that excess nerve energy not consumed by thought processes during sleep, had a cumulative action. Therefore, Hypnotic sleep resulted from an overabundance of unused nerve force.

BURCQ

In 1876, a French Physicist had experimented with Hypnosis for 25 years. On his deathbed, he asked his friend Claude Bernard to present his finding to the French Biological Society which formed a commission to investigate Hypnosis, and which published a favorable report.

CHARCOT

A French Neurologist in 1878 who became fascinated by Burcq's findings, Charcot and his students succeeded in proving that there are several stages of hypnotic sleep, and that the hypnotized subject is capable of manifesting varying symptoms in each stage. He also believed that Metalotherapy was the answer to the physician's prayers.

Those gentlemen all contributed knowledge and experience to the current process of Hypnosis through their work hundreds of years ago. We consider Mesmer the father of Hypnosis because he was the first one to publicly research the use of hypnosis-inducing activities. Based on our understanding of hypnosis today he was not engaging in hypnosis at that time but a form a hysteria-induced peer pressure. Nonetheless, his name is part of our language today as a testament to his work in the 1700's.

CHAPTER 4
HYPNOTIC INFLUENCES

We live in a world that is full of hypnotic influence. Hypnotherapists joke that our job isn't hypnotizing people; it's waking them up. Look around you next time you are outside your home and pay close attention to all the influencers you see. Look at the billboards and advertisements on buses, on airport shuttles, in store windows, on bus stop benches. Even inside your home, you are bombarded by your TV with non-stop commercials, your computer with ads for goods, services, software, more computers, bigger and better electronics and Web 2.0. Shop in a supermarket and you are deluged with store ads, flyers, coupons, bulletin boards with offers and more. We are constantly being hit with information. Some of that information has what I call hypnotic influence, capable of evoking an emotional response from viewers and sometimes creating a decision to take an action based on what was seen. That sure sounds hypnotic to me.

And if that's not enough, we are self-influencing all the time. Some of the self-influencing is positive and some is not. The typical human being engages in criticizing him/herself out loud to others and also engages in negative self-talk that seems to be on automatic pilot. Sometimes individuals have disagreements with other individuals that can erupt into interactions with high hypnotic influence, sometimes negative. Keep reading. You may see yourself in some of these situations.

Everyday Language

For the purposes of this discussion, let's think of Hypnosis as a behavior modification tool that involves either entering or inducing in others, an altered state that is concurrently a high learning state. It is more than that, however. Self Hypnosis or Hypnosis is a process that operates to some extent some of the time even when we are in a conscious state.

Here's what I mean by that. In the conscious state we are all affected to some degree by what we say, hear, see, and experience. For example, if you want to lose weight and you continue to refer to yourself out loud or silently to yourself as "Fatty" or some other derogatory term, you are listening to yourself and you are being affected by your words. If someone you love, respect or fear calls you 'Fatty", then the same dynamic is in effect. This isn't really "eyes open Hypnosis", but it can be a powerful programming event. Guard what you hear and what you say. Speak and hear only that which you want to show up in your life. I know that is easier said than done, but controlling your own mental programming is the ideal and it's achievable to a large extent.

I am often dismayed to hear the terrible things people say about themselves out loud. I can only shudder to think what they are saying silently to themselves. What degrading and critical words are being played in their heads? Don't be one of these people. Speak positively to yourself and to others about yourself and others. Remember, garbage in, garbage out.

Making the decision to speak only that which you want to show up in your life will go a long way to creating wonderful changes in your life and in the lives of those around you. If that's all you gain from this book, it will have been worth the purchase price.

I know that it's hard for an honest person to answer "I'm doing great" when asked, particularly when you're not. Just remember that in most cases, people don't really want to hear your troubles since they probably have some of their own. And sharing bad news can degenerate into a pity party really fast. Speak only that which you want to see in your life. Focus on the good in your life and speak only the good in your life which will in turn attract more good. Give it time, and you'll see results that may surprise you.

If you utilize what you are learning in this book, then the most powerful self-help tool in your personal toolbox will be self-hypnosis, whether for making quick behavioral changes or for upgrading existing beliefs. Going underneath the radar of your conscious mind to your subconscious mind means you're engaging the most creative, high learning brain state available to you. However, using self-hypnosis to build confidence, for example, when coupled with criticizing yourself out loud or silently is self-defeating. Listen carefully to what you say to others. If you find yourself downgrading yourself to others, stop! Also, become more aware of what others are saying to you; if others criticize you unkindly, don't put up with it. Glare, walk away or register your displeasure in some way. If you're in public and don't feel free to walk away, then say "cancel, cancel" to yourself when you hear someone say something that's derogatory about you or something that is negative in general. I know that sounds silly, but it works. Declare to yourself that your ears and your mind are a now a positivity zone. Speak, hear and think only the positive and naturally that's what you will attract.

I mention this only because in long-term relationships like Mother-Daughter, Father-Son, Boss-Employee, Sibling-

Sibling, we sometimes just tune things out. Your Mom starts ranting about your hair and your sloppy ways, and you just tune her out. Unfortunately, whether you are consciously listening or not, you are still taking in that information. Pay attention and edit what others say to you about you. Use "cancel, cancel" like a giant eraser ridding your mind of negative feedback or commentary. If you're in a relationship with someone who is critical, tell him or her to knock it off. Explain that you are no longer willing to listen to negativity directed at you. It will shock those in your life who engage in this behavior because some times others become so accustomed to speaking to you in this way that they're not even consciously aware that they're doing it. Humans habituate very easily. It takes about 17 days to form a habit. If your Mom has been criticizing you for 30 years, she's probably on auto-pilot. Same with spouses, bosses, etc. Therefore, changing that behavior may take some time, but continue to assert your right to be treated kindly and with respect.

Remember this. Those who either love you or claim to love

you should not be engaging in negative talk directed at you. Bosses who want employees to succeed do not berate them. Negative or unfair criticism creates negative behavior in the recipient. Criticism and slurs are not productive and they are generally not kind. Do not engage in unproductive, unkind language directed toward yourself or others. Offer courtesy to others and require the same back in return. While this is not classical Hypnosis, being spoken to critically or using self talk to berate yourself has powerful Hypnotic influence, so it is best to discourage it.

As a Clinical Hypnotherapist, I have worked with clients with weight issues and self esteem issues among many others. Clients reach their goals much more quickly when they eliminate negative self-talk and require the same kindness from others.

Here are some useful examples of negative speech that you will hear others say about themselves, once you really tune in to this issue:

A woman who wants to find a good loving relationship and yet continues to declare: "all the good men are taken." I have heard women say this repeatedly in a couple of hours of conversation. This is the best way to convince yourself you'll never find a good man. Strangely when I mentioned this habit to one woman, she said something like, "well, that's the way I keep the thought of finding a good man in my consciousness." Unfortunately, she's doing the opposite.

If you proclaim repeatedly, "I have no idea how I'm going to pay my mortgage this month", you are throwing highly emotional uncertainty into the stratosphere on the topic of the mortgage payment. Uncertainty boldly predicts an uncertain outcome. A Hypnosis client or yourself who wants to work on prosperity needs to proclaim and feel, "paying my mortgage this month is an absolute certainty". Again, some people seem to think the first statement is an invitation for the Universe to step in and fix the situation. Not so. A statement like "money flows easily to me" or "I always have what I need and what I want financially" is a positive, magnetizing money statement that is much more likely to produce positive results.

Weight loss is an interesting Hypnosis application and people say the darndest things on this topic. I have heard clients say in the pre-session interview things like, "I love donuts and I know that eating them makes me fat." Now that one makes me shudder because I know that if the client believes that donuts make her fat, then they do. You can be sure that in her Hypnosis session I included some language about eating the foods you love actually helps you to release excess weight.

One client said that she couldn't help being fat because of her genes. Everyone in her family is fat. I pointed out to her that the genome project failed miserably so we can't blame anything on genes anymore, but that in many cases food preparation and food preferences are shared by all or many family members. Fortunately, those are simply preferences or habits and can be changed to healthier ones.

Some believe that weight is determined by astrological signs or ethnic heritage. Well, the challenge here is that all Tauruses in the world are not heavy and 100% of any ethnicity is not overweight. That weight-related theory is statistically impossible. But if you the self-hypnosis subject or your client believes this to be true, then it is, at least for the client or for you. To counteract a belief like that, your self-hypnosis session should be replete with suggestions that you are free of any limiting beliefs about ethnicity or astrology as it relates to your weight.

Self Talk

Self Talk is the "tape" I referenced earlier that plays in your head (usually on autopilot) that berates and criticizes you, pointing out flaws and ill-advised actions. Earlier I mentioned this topic, which can act as an impediment to your creating successful Self-Hypnosis sessions that produce fast, permanent change for you.

Most people probably know what I mean by self talk but for

those who don't, it's simply a "tape" that play automatically in the heads of most people that involves the replaying of an upsetting conversation or personal interaction that hurt you or that made you feel bad. Self-talk can also be the inner tape that criticizes the self for stupidity, foolish actions and other such situations with the occasional hateful thought directed toward others. Individuals don't decide to play this inner tape; it's probably a leftover from childhood. I think of it as the self internalization of the critical voice of the primary parent. I'll tell you what I told myself years ago when I finally got that inner voice to shut up. If someone hurts you or scares you, that's a shame. If you repeat it over and over again in your head hurting yourself or scaring yourself again and again, that's just plain foolish. Being hurt the first time was bad enough. Why replay it again and again? Why injure yourself? There will always be those who will say bad things about or to you, given the opportunity. Why would you add to that by saying bad things about yourself out loud or in your head? You need to be your own best friend. You need to be the loving, patient parent you may not have had. Be that parent to yourself today. Promise yourself to work on stopping that voice in your head. Promise yourself to be the only one who programs your mind and always program it positively and kindly. You have the power to make your mind your sanctuary. It can be a place of silent contemplation for making decisions, finding solutions or creating something. When you eliminate that hateful angry inner voice, you will discover in its place a secret garden of quiet contemplation and peace.

I hope those of you who still engage in self talk cut yourselves free of that hurtful and damaging habit. You'll feel your general mood lift considerably once you do and it will speed your progress with Self Hypnosis sessions. With Self Hypnosis, you have the power to heal your hurts and improve every aspect of your life. Do what you can to support that process. Speak kindly to yourself silently and out loud and that change alone will improve your life immeasurably.

Eyes Open Hypnosis

Human beings are learning machines. We learn good things and sometimes we learn unfortunate or negative things. The only constant is that we learn 24-7. I believe that even dreams can also be learning experiences; I have read references to this possibility which makes sense to me, in that we are in alpha and deeper brain states in sleep which support the learning process. I know personally that the emotions from a dream can stay with me for an entire day.

Our brains crave stimulation. Do you remember the last time you went someplace entirely new for the first time? Do you remember the feeling of your eyes taking in all the brand new sights and sounds, almost hungry for entirely new information? I do. Going to Europe for the first time, my eyes gulped up all the new scenes, clothing styles of the people, streets, buildings, cars and more. Most of what I saw and heard was entirely different from what my eyes were used to seeing. All that new information trained my brain in new ways and expanded my perception of the world.

Meeting a new person and exploring the possibility of a new relationship is exciting for lots of reasons but one of those reasons is that he or she is an entirely new sight complete with new sounds and new points of view. Learning "him/her" is fun because it's such a new and therefore stimulating experience for the mind, body and the soul. Listening completely to everything he/she says probably increases the pleasure because we listen less completely when the same familiar people are saying the same familiar things. With those people we know well, there is no need for rapt attention as we have already "learned" them.

Because of this yen for learning and need for visual and auditory stimulation, we can end up being much more open to outside programming than we would consciously choose to be.

Here's what I mean. As a human being, you are a genius with a big, hungry brain. If you work at things that you don't enjoy or that are highly repetitive and if you feel frustrated in your work situation, a lot of that may be due to the lack of visual and intellectual stimulation. Your body and your brain may be tired of the same place, the same people, and the same work. Of course you're frustrated and thank God that you are. If you weren't, then you wouldn't be human. Besides, you are in the process of learning that you can change almost any situation in your life. Finding a more meaningful way to earn a living isn't that hard to accomplish once you put your mind to it.

The lack of adequate visual stimulation can lead us to silly behaviors that most of us have engaged in, like reading a dog-eared children's magazine while waiting in the doctor's office. The same need for stimulation that leads us to read a child's magazine opens the door to "eyes open" Hypnosis or Hypnotic influences which are all around us, often affecting our behavior and sometimes our decisions.

Hypnotic influences are happening around us all the time. Here are some examples:

You're sitting on the sofa watching TV laughing at a

comedy, open and happy. Your husband comes in and starts yelling at you while standing above you about your leaving the car lights on again and the battery being dead again. You're startled and looking up at him above your natural horizon. He's upset which heightens the emotional impact of what he's saying and catapults you into a new situation. He's telling you that you must be pretty dumb to keep doing this. Because of your elevated eye placement (20% above your natural horizon activates an alpha brain state), the combination of his emotion and your startled fear reaction, can catapult you into a spontaneous "eyes open" Hypnosis and start "learning" "that you're dumb."

This is not the same level of Hypnosis you achieve in a quiet place with a good Hypnosis script. That ideal situation creates a higher learning state than this emotionally charged one. However, in this emotional attack situation, learning is likely occurring about your alleged lack of intelligence, your lack of safety in your own home, your ability to trust your husband, etc. Learning on some level is occurring. And that's the point. Eyes Open Hypnosis happens a lot of the time to most of us. When in the above situation from now on, don't become passive and accept that "information". Get up, move away from the anger, and close your mind. I hope that the above has never happened to you and never will, but the same and worse happens to people all the time.

I hope you can't recall this, but if you had angry parents, you may remember one or both of them leaning down, still way above your eye level, yelling at you about something. If you concentrate for a moment on that experience, you can probably recall sort of "going away" mentally to avoid the upset. Even in that "going away" state which can become a form of hypnosis, learning was occurring.

Hypnosis occurs a lot of the time. When you are watching TV, particularly if the TV is placed in an elevated location above your natural horizon, your mind is learning as you're watching and it's possible for you will enter a light state of Hypnosis. If you watch violent shows, you can be taking in fear, upset, anxiety et cetera and accepting it as part of your reality.

If you go to church and have a pastor who is a "hell fire and damnation "type, you may be taking in some subliminal information that isn't helpful to you. It's harder for you to evaluate the information when you are entering into or are in a light state of Hypnosis. This is not a criticism of ministers or pastors or that style of ministering. This behavior can induce a light state of Hypnosis which is why I'm mentioning it now. Having someone in a raised voice declaring your perfection, brilliance, and absolute inner and outer beauty would be a good thing. Anyone promising loudly that you will end up in Hell for so many reasons is probably not a good thing, only because the energy and passion of the speaker will likely kick you into a high learning state.

Many computer desks used to feature an elevated platform for the monitor which again caused your eyes to elevate, making you more susceptible to an unintended learning situation. There's a lot of information online that isn't necessarily anything you want to habituate into your life. Popular music can induce a form of hypnosis. If there's a steady beat of any sort, that beat can entrain the brain to focus on the message and to enter an unintentional hypnotic learning state. As you know, the messages shared in some popular music today are not what you want to entrain in your mind or in your kids' minds.

When watching movies or TV at home or movies in the movie theater, if the screen is elevated 20 degrees or more above your normal eye level, you can again thrown into unintended learning state, especially with violent movies or television. Will watching these movies in a lightly hypnotized state cause you to become a killer? No. However, it may persuade you that violence is a normal part of life and that belief may introduce violence into your life in some other way.

Remember, we've discussed the importance of choosing the learning experiences that will benefit you. Watching violent films and TV shows opens your mind to the possibility of violence in your life. Conversely, watching "happily ever after" shows is a better form of mental programming and opens your mind to the possibility of happily ever after for you.

The components of Eyes Open Hypnosis are much the same as the components for Hypnosis. And they are:

-An authority figure or in the case of self-hypnosis, a trusted voice.

-Misdirected attention, as in someone yelling at you or in self-hypnosis, a boring/relaxing induction.

-Expectation, such as heightened emotion or in self-hypnosis, trusting yourself.

-Belief. Unfortunately, we are programmed to believe what we see and what we hear. We can exercise control over that process when we are in a fully alert state. It is less easy to do so in a light alpha state.

So what's the message here? It's not that the world is a

dangerous place with tons of people trying to influence or control you. However, it is a place full of hypnotic influences that you can control or erase to a large extent. The purpose of this section is merely to help you to understand that hypnosis is more a part of your life than you may have known, and that you have the power to choose the sort of mental programming you will accept. It's also important for parents reading this book to understand how compelling almost every interaction with their children is for those kids. Learning and Eyes Open Hypnosis are part of our daily lives. Choose the type of learning you wish to share and also the type you wish to experience. Then reinforce those standards in your life and in the lives of those you love.

Conversational Hypnosis

I only mention this because it's all over the internet so I wanted to cover it. The premise seems to suggest that you can fully hypnotize people without them noticing it. Wow, that would really be something wouldn't it? In reality, what really happens in "conversational hypnosis" has a lot more with NLP than it does with Hypnosis.

The process referred to online as Conversational Hypnosis uses Neuro-linguistic Programming prompts to create an immediate sense of intimacy by subtly suggesting what you want the other person to do. NLP involves "pacing" him (speaking more slowly to calm him), mirroring the other person's body position (if he has his left elbow on the table, you put your left elbow on the table, etc) and generally mirroring him in as many ways as you can. If you had some advance notice of the type of person you'd be dealing with, you'd want to dress like him, go to a restaurant that he would like, order the same food and drink that he did, etc.

Conversational Hypnosis attempts to remove any barriers that impede forming a quick bond with another person, in order to sell him something, persuade him to do something, or get something from him. You are attempting to create an almost instant intimacy with this person. Even though this process relies on NLP prompts, the process can become somewhat hypnotic for both the person engaging in NLP use and the person who is on the receiving end of this process.

Street Hypnosis

I will only spend a moment or two on this one. On YouTube.com, you can watch roving bands of individuals going up to others sitting peacefully somewhere-on a park bench, a sofa, a chair-and the alleged "street hypnotist" wraps his or her arm around the individual's neck and puts pressure on an acupressure point that causes the individual to lose consciousness. At the same time, the "street hypnotist" is seen to be whispering in the person's ear. This is not hypnosis; it's assault.

CHAPTER 5
SELF HYPNOSIS EXPLAINED

We've been talking a lot about aspects and types of Hypnosis and Self Hypnosis but what is Hypnosis really and how does it work? This is a short question with a long answer, so let's get started.

First of all, Self Hypnosis involved the same person playing both the role of Hypnotist and the role of client. The terms Hypnosis and Self Hypnosis in terms of techniques and methods are synonymous, so when we speak of Hypnosis which is the vehicle or process that drives Self Hypnosis, we are also referring to the particular form of Hypnosis we've chosen to focus on in this book, which is Self Hypnosis.

Let's look again at the Hypnotic formula that we teach in the NEIH training program:

Hypnosis = Misdirected Attention + Belief + Expectation

After reading this, I'm pretty sure you are still wondering what Hypnosis is. Let me explain. An individual in a conscious state prior to entering the hypnotic state usually has lots on his mind. Money worries, relationship worries, endless self talk; in other words, he is alive and conscious but likely up in his head, figuring things out or worrying about things. This isn't a criticism; brains need lots of stimulation. A brain just sitting there in your head in a quiet room will come up with something to think about in a short period of time.

Someone who wants to hypnotize the above mentioned individual will need to misdirect his attention to get him free of that inner monologue. In Hypnosis, the misdirection takes the form of a Hypnosis induction. The induction does a couple of things. It misdirects the client's inner focus and it bores him quickly and well. The combination of a hypnotic induction offered in a slow, cadenced way using repetitive phrases is so incredibly boring that the subject or client just lets go of the conscious state and relaxes into a hypnotic state with the assistance of the cadenced induction.

Remember how you have felt sitting in a lecture where the speaker is speaking too slowly for you or sharing information that has no value to you? Remember how you sort of drifted away, thought about other things for awhile and then struggled not to fall asleep? That's the way a good hypnotic induction works. It ceases to be interesting pretty quickly and then lulls the client or self into a pre-sleep state that is ideally an alpha brain state. As the induction continues, the individual enters more fully into a hypnotic state. Whether we're talking about Hypnosis or Self-Hypnosis, the mechanism is the same. We take an alert, sometimes anxious client or self, bore him, and then induce him into the ideal state of Hypnosis in which behavior or belief modification occurs. If you're thinking that this sounds awfully simple, it is. There is no rocket science involved here. Getting yourself or a friend or client into the ideal state of Hypnosis is easy if you follow our suggested steps.

Okay, so now you've completely induced Hypnosis in yourself or a client. What comes next? Once you are in the appropriate state, then the behavioral modification portion of the Hypnosis session begins. At NEIH, we suggest that our students use the following components of a complete Hypnosis session:

Master Hypnosis Induction
Path (NLP Prompts)
Behavior Modification
Path Return
Count-Up Script

We include the Path portion of the above session outline because it gives you the opportunity to invoke the subconscious mind's genius to facilitate the session. The Path is about 3 minutes long and it serves an important function in the session. Here's why we use it. Research has shown that individuals in a full state of Hypnosis or deep Meditation can not differentiate between a suggested experience and an actual experience. Adding Neuro-Linguistic Programming prompts, as we do in the Path script, can considerably improve the quality and outcome of the

Hypnosis session. By adding suggested sights, sounds and kinesthetic verbal prompts as we do in the Path portion of the Hypnosis session, the hypnotist can increase the client or the self's sense of reality about the experience. Using the Path also engages the subconscious mind early in the process. You will remember reading in a previous chapter that in Hypnosis, we engage the subject's subconscious mind to create a reality experience for him/her. The more real the experience seems, the greater the benefits from the session. And some sessions can seem very real to hypnotic subjects.

In the late 1990's, NEIH conducted an attended Certification seminar in the Southern US. One of the students was a really lovely, compliant, easy-going lady. She was a pleasure to have in class and we all instantly liked her. During a practice session that I conducted with the group, she appeared to get a sunburn while we were "on the beach" which is my preferred backdrop for the behavior modification component of a Hypnosis session. After the group came out of session, I didn't comment on her "sunburn" because I was sure I was imagining it and I wanted to see if the rest of the group would notice it. A student in the class finally asked our red-faced student if she thought that she had gotten sun-burned on the beach. The student, who had been touching her face repeatedly after coming out of the session, said "I feel like I do have sunburn." She was a very fair-complexioned person, blonde and her face was getting redder and redder. She excused herself, went into the bathroom and came out with a shocked look on her face. She said, "I should have thought to put on some suntan lotion" at which point we all laughed. The "sunburn" was gone after lunch, but this woman's experience made a big impression on all of us.

That was the most dramatic immediate physical result of a Hypnosis session I've experienced. There have been other unexpected occurrences such as a very serious, buttoned-up student coming out of a group past life regression, undoing his tie, rolling up his sleeves and asking another student for a piece of gum which he loudly popped throughout the rest of the afternoon's class while cracking jokes. His behavior was so out of character with the person we'd become accustomed to seeing that we were doing double-takes all afternoon. He maintained a happy, casual demeanor throughout the rest of the 5-Day Intensive. We never saw him wear a necktie again. He went home, did 20 Hypnosis weigh loss sessions that week with his counseling practice clients and lost 10 lbs himself that week, without conducting a weight loss Self Hypnosis session on himself. You just have to say it. The human mind is an astonishing gift and Hypnosis is like the bow on top of the package. Put the two together and wow! Miracles happen.

So let's circle back to the topic for this chapter. What is hypnosis? Let me give you some adjectives to describe Hypnosis such as miraculous, pleasant, effective, relaxing, healing, easy, quick, and fun.

Let's recall the Hypnotic formula mentioned earlier in this chapter.

Hypnosis= Misdirected Attention + Belief+ Expectation

That's certainly the best way to get someone into Hypnosis. The actual experience of Hypnosis itself is a dream-like state that a well-trained practitioner of Hypnosis creates in a client or in himself. Achieving this hypnotic state allows the individual to enter a high-learning state in which he enjoys enhance suggestibility. While the client or subject is in that state, the Hypnotist or Self-Hypnotist creates suggestions based on what he either knows about himself or what he has learned from interviewing the client. This process helps the client/self to create behavioral changes or to update his/her belief systems almost instantly in most cases. How? We will cover that in the next chapter.

Before we move to the next chapter, I'd like to return for a moment to the Path portion of a Hypnosis script. The structure of the Hypnosis session as we teach it at NEIH is composed of the Master Hypnosis Induction, the Path, the Beach (our behavior modification component), then the Return Path, and the Count-Up (the stairs) Script component if stairs or numbers were used in the Master Induction and then back to the present time and place. When we get to the

Induction chapter, we will go over this in more detail. At this point, we will focus on the Path for a moment.

The Path is actually just that, a rustic graveled path in the country than runs along in front of a pasture with grazing brown and white cows, a red barn, a field of daisies, and a duck pond with ducks splashing in the water. There are trees lining the path, so that walking along the path allows the client or the self to move in and out of the sun and shade, experience a light breeze and enjoy the temperature which is around 70 degrees Fahrenheit. Including this virtual experience with your session or your client's allows for the introduction of all 3 of the NLP communication and learning styles: auditory, visual and kinesthetic. In the session, we suggest that the client/self can hear the leaves rustling in the trees, the birds chirping overhead, feel a cool breeze on his face as well as the dappling sun on the top of his head. As we describe these scenes, the client or yourself has the opportunity to anchor those colors, images, sounds and feelings in his mind to make the process of visualizing the images that you suggest from the Hypnosis session script, easier and more real.

There's more to the Path script, but you get the idea. We are striving to make this as real as possible for the subject by engaging all 3 of the primary learning/communication styles. We have included the Path script along with the Master Hypnosis Inductions so that you can add it to your sessions as is or modify it as you choose.

Now we'll move on to the next chapter and explore how Hypnosis works.

CHAPTER 6
HOW SELF HYPNOSIS WORKS

Again, how does Hypnosis really work? This is another simple question with a few complex answers. The first answer pretty much sums it all up. We really don't know. The scientific community concedes that Hypnosis works because of demonstrated results, but doesn't know how. That's not surprising since there is no absolute certainty about exactly how the brain works either. Researchers have mapped large areas of the brain and know what aspects of feeling or functioning that certain areas control but as far as fully understanding the human brain, we're not there yet.

Along with the brain, the mind shares the designation as the last great frontier of the human body.

Most of us have used brain and mind synonymously but we now know that "mind" is not limited to the brain, but rather it's the intelligence contained in every cell of the human body. Cells demonstrate cellular intelligence in their ability to communicate with each other. Not just to manage cooperative body functions, but also to communicate danger and to influence the behavior of other cells. This book is not about spirituality but allow me to inject just a bit of that now. I believe that cellular intelligence is the God-Spark within us and also what we call the Soul. Regardless of what you call it, cellular intelligence exists and exerts a profound influence on your body's behavior. So let's get back to your brain for a moment.

Your brain is almost but not completely divided into two halves. We refer to them as the right brain or right hemisphere and the left brain or the left hemisphere. The right brain is generally known to be the creative side of the brain as we discussed earlier. The left brain is generally known to be the logical side of your brain. An interesting point is that the left brain has dominance over the right side of your body and the right brain has dominance over the left side of your body. That's called cross-dominance.

There is a small "bridge" that connects the 2 halves of your brain which allows communication between the 2 hemispheres. Individuals who sustain head injuries that sever the connection to the right and left hemispheres lose the ability to function properly.

As relevant to this discussion, I'd like to congratulate you on having such an excellent brain. Our brains are amazing. I suspect that everyone you know is a genius whether their IQs are 140+ or not. An IQ score of 140+ is the going standard for genius in the US. Well, you can forget that number because it really doesn't apply in truth. I believe it accurately measures the extent to which an individual is able to use his brain successfully. I believe that individuals we call geniuses use a tiny portion more than the average individual does. Researchers have shown that the average human being uses 5-6% of his brain capacity. A genius uses 8-10% of his brain capacity. That means the brightest among us still uses less than 10% of available brain power. So, let me ask you this. If you have a Million dollars in the bank, but only spend $2000 a month, are you still a

Millionaire? Well, of course you are. If you personally are using less than 8% of your available brain power, then logic dictates that you are a brilliant person, most likely a genius. Look how much you've accomplished using the tiniest portion of your available brain power.

Think about it. Yes, in some ways man has made a mess of things, but nonetheless, using 5-6% of available brain power, we've built cities, town, airplanes, trains, cars, industry, computers, telephones, cell phones, television, medical cures, etc.

You can only imagine what would be possible if the typical human used 10% of his brain power. I believe sincerely that given how little brain power humans have used to create what would have been considered miracles 100 years ago, the only logical conclusion is that we are lazy geniuses who haven't yet figured out how to access all that extra real estate just sitting there up in our heads. But we will; I'm confident of that. So, whether you think you're smart or dumb, you're wrong. You and every one you know is a genius. You have the opportunity to squeeze more brain power out of that head of yours because the power is definitely there. But like the frugal millionaire, whether you're using all of your assets or not, you still own them, just as you own that remarkably valuable real estate that sits, mostly unused in the upper half of your cranium.

As we mentioned before, mind and brain are 2 separate aspects of the human body. Mind is everywhere and the brain is in the head. In Hypnosis, we work with the subconscious mind which is primarily paired with the right brain. The right brain is focused on creative activities and subjective thoughts and experiences. The left brain as you will remember is focused on logical activities, objective thinking and activities; the left brain is always associated with the conscious mind.

Getting back to your mind, you have a conscious mind and a subconscious mind. The conscious mind is in charge of maintaining homeostasis in your body and your life. The subconscious mind is child-like, subjective and experiential.

The subconscious mind understands symbols, colors, images and other non-linear, non-verbal communication. I believe it's this part of the mind that makes adjustments in your thinking when someone hurts your feelings or when you injure yourself. I believe that the list of acceptable activities, experiences and people is maintained and modified by the subconscious mind. The subconscious mind learns all the time, just like a child, being influenced by every experience, sound, symbol and feeling. So you can see how Hypnosis when moving beneath the conscious mind's editor, can more easily access the highly suggestible, and easily influenced subconscious mind. And that is the crux of how hypnosis works. By inducing a client or self into a highly suggestible and highly accessible subconscious mind state, the conscious mind is over-ridden and change occurs more easily.

If at this point, you are asking yourself why we have to get beneath the radar of the conscious mind, let me explain again. The conscious mind is like the inner mother and the subconscious mind is like the inner child. The inner mother's job is to keep the inner child in line, maintain order and keep life moving along in an orderly fashion. This is great because without the conscious mind keeping things working properly, there would be chaos. So we need the conscious mind to do what it does, except when it's time to change things. The conscious mind's job is to avoid change at almost any cost. As we mentioned before, the primary responsibility of the conscious mind is maintaining homeostasis or keeping everything exactly as it is, which is the exact opposite of change. Have you ever wondered why it can be so hard to make simple changes in your life? You make a decision that you feel is important and two days later, things are right back to where they were before you made the decision. Habit is a powerful tool of the conscious mind and a way of maintaining things just as they are.

The mechanism we use once we've accessed the Subconscious Mind is to create a utopian "reality" during the Behavior Modification component of a full Hypnosis session. You offer your Subconscious Mind an appealing new "virtual reality" alternative which the Subconscious Mind embraces and ratifies, replacing the old "reality" with this new, more appealing one. It's like replacing outdated software. When your brain reboots after the Hypnosis session, it's like your computer rebooting after you update existing software.

Fortunately, with a boring and nicely cadenced Hypnosis induction, the skilled Self-Hypnotist can distract or misdirect his/her conscious mind and slip beneath that gatekeeper to the change-loving subconscious mind. That's how hypnosis works and you can see now when I said that Hypnosis isn't rocket science, I wasn't kidding. The tools you need to create great Self Hypnosis sessions are right here in this book, just waiting for you to move forward into actually using this exciting process to create dynamic changes in your life. If you follow the suggestions we offer you in this book, and use the included inductions and sessions, you can get off to a great start by making the desired changes and creating your own custom sessions.

Who Is Using Hypnosis?

Probably more people than you think. At NEIH, we train predominantly but not exclusively, mental health practitioners, chiropractors, social workers, yoga instructors, massage therapists, life coaches, personal coaches, naturopaths, holistic counselors and more. They work professionally with all types of people. And while not everyone is using Hypnosis, you might be amazed to find out how many people do use Hypnosis to improve their lives.

Professional athletes use Hypnosis to embed the images of the perfect game into their minds and into their muscle memory. A very famous golfer has created his "perfect" game by splicing together selected video from many games and he is alleged to watch it before every game. There's also at least one famous pro tennis player who does the same. Researchers have determined that watching the perfect game is 33% more effective at improving the game than the actual physical practice. That statistic strikes me as pretty amazing.

NEIH trained a woman in New England as a Certified Hypnotherapist who works with professional hockey players. We last talked years ago, and her team was having an amazing season in part as a result of the work she was doing with them.

Stage performers of many types are said to use Hypnosis to get them pumped up and ready to put on a high energy performance. Public speakers use Hypnosis for similar reasons. When you're a highly paid public speaker or performer you are expected to be "on" whether your foot hurts or you had a fight with your spouse, etc. Hypnosis can help clear away the emotional debris and get the mind focused on the job at hand.

For those of you who haven't yet experienced Hypnosis, there is a really nice surprise for you at the end of the book. It's an opportunity to get a Free Hypnosis session so that you can use to begin to entrain your brain and to experience Hypnosis as a subject before you experience it as both the subject and the hypnotist.

Remember, your mind and brain is limitless. Hypnosis helps you connect with your genius subconscious mind to upgrade beliefs and then make behavioral changes that you desire. You will find that adding Self Hypnosis to you life is healing, fun and potentially game-changing.

CHAPTER 7
MASTER HYPNOSIS INDUCTIONS

These Master Induction scripts are the core tools for creating Hypnosis sessions, taking yourself or a client from the waking state to a medium state of hypnosis.

We have included a classic Master Hypnosis Induction as well as some of our newer favorite Inductions.

NEIH Classic Master Hypnosis Induction

This is a longer induction and takes about 30 minutes to transition from the waking state to a full medium state of Hypnosis. It features a "big relax" at the beginning, then the classic Count-down, the Path, the Behavior Modification segment (set on a beach), Reverse Path and Count-Up segment that brings you back to the waking state. The dots and commas are here to indicate extended pauses, helping you to cadence easily.

[Begin Script]

As you continue to breathe deeply, I would like you to allow your body to become more and more relaxed. And as your body becomes more and more relaxed, you can feel a tingling on the top of your head. Feel the top of your head becoming more and more relaxed. As you continue to become more and more relaxed, perfectly at peace, perfectly at ease, perfectly safe, and perfectly secure, your relaxation deepens.

And as you continue to become more and more relaxed, you feel that wonderful sense of relaxation traveling down the back of your head; you may have a sense of warmth and a sense of tingling as you become more and more relaxed, more and more at peace, welcoming this gentle and warm relaxation that is filling your body.

As you continue to become more and more relaxed, you can feel this sense of relaxation moving down the front of your face, as you feel the tiny muscles around your eyes relaxing, and the corners of your mouth relaxing, and your jaw relaxing. Throughout this process, you feel your eyelids becoming heavier and heavier as you become more perfectly relaxed and more perfectly at peace.

As you become more and more relaxed, you feel yourself breathing more deeply, you feel yourself taking deep relaxing breaths of air, as you fill your lungs with oxygen and your body, with a deepening sense of relaxation.

As you continue to become more and more relaxed, you feel this wonderful sense of calm and peace moving down your neck relaxing your shoulders and down your chest. As you feel yourself becoming more and more relaxed, you find it is so easy to breathe deeply, filling your lungs with life-giving oxygen as you become more and more relaxed.

As you become more and more relaxed, you feel this relaxation moving down the front of your body, relaxing your hips and your knees as it moves down your body, all the way to your feet. As you continue to breathe deeply, you can feel the bottoms of your feet tingling and becoming perfectly relaxed.

As you become more and more perfectly relaxed, you feel the relaxation moving down your back and down the backs of your legs until all of you is completely relaxed.

As you continue to breathe deeply, becoming more and more relaxed, perfectly at ease, perfectly at peace, you feel yourself moving forward toward a wide set of well-lit stairs. They remind you of a large beautiful set of stone steps you saw in an art museum at some point in time, and you feel yourself looking forward to walking down these stairs. You feel safe as you think about moving down these well-lighted stairs.

As you find yourself moving toward these stairs, you have a sense of anticipation. You are looking forward to moving down these stairs, and you feel perfectly safe, perfectly secure, as you continue forward.

As you move down the steps, I will count backwards from 10-1. When you reach one, you will be perfectly relaxed, in your own natural state of relaxation. Counting down now.... [You will repeat the phrases shown below for each step, 4-5 times very slowly, which will allow you to spend about 5 minutes at each step.]

~Number 10 - Feeling good, feeling fine, perfectly safe, perfectly secure; as you continue to breathe deeply, you feel yourself surrendering to the deep and perfect relaxation that is filling your body. And you feel fine, perfectly safe, perfectly secure...moving down...going deeper and deeper.

~Number 9 - As you continue to move down the stairs, you feel yourself becoming more and more relaxed, perfectly at peace, feeling good, feeling fine, perfectly safe, perfectly secure and as you continue to breathe deeply, you feel yourself surrendering to the deep and perfect relaxation that is filling your body. And you feel fine, perfectly safe, perfectly secure...moving down...going deeper and deeper.

~Number 8 - As you continue to move down the stairs, you feel yourself becoming more and more relaxed, perfectly at peace, feeling good, feeling fine, perfectly safe, perfectly secure and as you continue to breathe deeply, you feel yourself surrendering to the deep and perfect relaxation that is filling your body. And you feel fine, perfectly safe, perfectly secure...moving down...going deeper and deeper. Every sound that you hear causes you to go deeper and deeper, deeper and deeper, deeper and deeper.

~Number 7 - Feeling good, feeling fine, perfectly safe, perfectly secure, as you continue to breathe deeply, you feel yourself surrendering to the deep and perfect relaxation that is filling your body. And you feel fine, perfectly safe, perfectly secure...moving down...going deeper and deeper. Every number you hear causes you to go deeper and deeper. As you continue to move down the stairs, you feel yourself becoming more and more relaxed, perfectly at peace, feeling good, feeling fine, perfectly safe, and perfectly secure. As you continue to breathe deeply, you feel yourself surrendering to the deep and perfect relaxation that is filling your body. And you feel fine, perfectly safe, perfectly secure...moving down...going deeper and deeper. Every sound that you hear causes you to go deeper and deeper, deeper and deeper, deeper and deeper.

~Number 6 - Just continue to repeat #7 shown above, repeating the same phrases 3-5 times for each number through #2.

~Number 5 – [Repeat #7 phrases 3-4 times]

~Number 4 - Ditto

~Number 3 – Ditto

~ Number 2 - Ditto

~ Number 1 - As you continue to breathe deeply, you feel yourself becoming more and more relaxed, perfectly at peace, perfectly at ease, perfectly safe, perfectly secure, happy and feeling fine. You are now at the perfect state of relaxation.

[Transition into the Path Script]

The Path Script Component

[Begin Script]

And as you reach the bottom of the stairs, you find yourself in a large round room with floor to ceiling windows, and you see the sunlight streaming thru the windows, warming the flagstone floor.

And up ahead you see a large oak door; you feel drawn to the door and have a sense of anticipation at the thought of moving through this doorway.

You move forward and grasp the brass door handle, and pull the door open, and as you do, you hear the hinges squeak as you move thru the doorway into a beautiful pastoral area.

And as you look around, you see on your left a large, red barn with a shiny metal roof. You see the sun glancing off the roof, and you are amazed at how bright the red of the barn is. As you continue to look, you see 2 black and white cows grazing contentedly in the pasture in front of the barn. As you watch them, you have a sense of their peace and contentment, and you find yourself taking on some of that peace and contentment as you walk along the path.

As you move along the path you hear the sound of the gravel crunching under your feet and you feel the cool breeze against your skin... you hear the birds in the trees above your head, you smell the flowers growing alongside the gravel path... you hear the sound of the breeze as it moves through the trees... you feel the roughness of the gravel on the path through your shoes, and you hear the sounds the cows are making as they eat the grass growing in the pasture.

As you continue to move along the path, you see a duck pond up ahead on the right, and as you look you can see 2 ducks playing in the pond, you hear the sounds they make as they play in the water, and you can see how much fun they are having as they play in the water... as you continue to watch them, you notice to the left of the pond a field of daisies, and you see how the white and yellow of their flowers contrast with the green of the grass; you see how beautiful and magical this place is.

As you continue to move along the path, you hear the sound of the birds in the trees, and you feel the breeze against your skin, and you feel the sun warming your head and your shoulders as you move along the path.

And as you move along the path, you feel the crunch of the gravel under your feet, and you hear the sounds of the birds in the trees and you feel the breeze against your skin, and you have a sense of the beauty of this magical place.

As you continue to move along the path, you notice that the path is changing to sand and as you continue to look around you notice that you are in a beautiful beach area.

[Transition into the Behavior Modification Script Component]

Behavior Modification Script Component

[The Beach - You can substitute other locations for the Behavioral Modification beach location, but try to choose a place with lots of color, activity and people. This is where you will insert one of the included hypnosis session scripts to create your hypnosis session.]

[Begin Script]

And as you look around you see the ocean on the left... and you see children playing at the water's edge... they are playing with a large red beach ball...they're laughing and playing and as you look at them, you notice that they are wearing brightly colored bathing suits.

And as you continue along the beach, you hear the sounds of seagulls, and you see them swooping and diving over the ocean, you feel the warmth of the sun against your skin; you hear the sounds of children laughing... as you continue to move along the beach.

And as you continue to move along the beach, you feel the sun warming your head, you notice your clothes feel loose, and that you feel strong, and confident, happy to be alive, and happy to be you, as you move along the path.

And as you continue to move along the path, you smell the salt from the ocean, you hear happy beach sounds, and you are glad to be here, and happy to be so strong, confident, healthy, and happy, as you move along the beach.

[To create a custom hypnosis session, this is where you would add your 7-9 custom suggestions in conversational form as you continue to walk along the beach, commenting on the people, sights, sounds, and smells.]

[After the Behavior Modification portion of your script is complete, reverse the Path, just as if you were there, and then use the Count-Up Script component to return to the present moment and time.]

[End Script]

Relax Master Hypnosis Induction

This induction can be as long or short as you want it to be, so customize it to suit your hypnotic style; I've found that about 15 minutes of this Relax induction works perfectly for me.

I've begun experimenting with scripts without stairs or a numbered descent for awhile now. I've become a bit tired personally of the count-down, although I have no idea why. I really like this simple, repetitive script which I find very effective for achieving a full medium state of hypnosis in about half the time of the Classic Master Induction.

This is an extremely boring (therefore perfect!) script that's great for left brain people, probably because you're not saying anything that they can have an inner argument with.

When you complete the session, do a quick count-up to bring yourself or the client back to the present place and time.

[Begin Script]

Take a deep breath and imagine that you can feel a sense of deepening relaxation begin to develop throughout your body. Now imagine that the sense of relaxation starts on the top of your head as a small spot. Allow yourself to imagine that spot increasing in size and sliding down the back of your head (pause) and now down your face relaxing your eyelids, your jaw, and your neck and all the way down the front of your body. You feel growing warmth and perhaps a slight tingling as your body relaxes more fully.

As we continue, you take another deep breath and then you RELAX.

[BIG PAUSE - 20-30 seconds]

And RELAX. (Drag out the word)

[BIG PAUSE - 20-30 seconds]

And RELAX

And so on for another 13 minutes

[End Script]

Transition into your Hypnosis Session Script and then count-up 10-1 using the suggestions included in the Count-Up Script.

River Quick Master Induction Hypnosis

Read this script very slowly with exaggerated pauses every 3 or 6 words. Always start with your eyes closed in a comfortable chair at a quiet time. Cell phones off. The dots in this script indicate the suggested pauses.

[Begin Script]

As you sit back and breathe deeply… you remember a

time… when you were younger… a child really… without a care and on that day… you were floating peacefully… in the water… weightless… drifting… easy… contented... carried along gently… by the water… drifting away… drifting away… peaceful… weightless… free as a bird. You may have been in a swimming pool… it may have been a lake… it may have been a river... it doesn't matter… you remember the lovely times you had there… playing in the water… floating in the water…

Imagine a perfect day and on this day… imagine that you were floating… on an inflatable raft down a gentle… meandering river… feeling the buoyancy… of the water… gently lifting you… carrying you… supporting you… as you drift away… floating weightless… in the water… loving that feeling of peace… contented… effortless pleasure… feeling your muscles relax completely… feeling your breathing change… slowing… slowing… deeper and deeper… allowing yourself to drift in and out… of a perfect… dream-like state… floating… safe… secure… protected… down and down… the river you float… you drift… easy and gentle... happy and peaceful. As you listen... to my voice... your mind relaxes... easily and peacefully. Effortlessly... deeper and deeper... deeper and deeper, you drift into a lovely sleep-like state.

As you continue... to drift... on that slow... and gentle river... if you allow yourself... you can hear the water lapping gently... moving downward toward the lake... you enjoy the feeling... of the sun... peeking through the canopy... of leaves overhead... protecting you... from the heat of the day. The sun gently... caresses your skin... and you hear... the sounds of birds chirping... the leaves rustling... in the gentle breeze... as you drift away going deeper... and deeper... into that easy... peaceful place... your mind at peace... cares all washed away... gently rocking in the peaceful water... as you allow yourself... to go deeper... and deeper... into that dream-like state... of perfect contentment... perfectly safe... perfectly at ease... Nurtured... protected and secure... feeling free of any concerns.

As you continue to breathe gently... you feel yourself slipping away into a peaceful, happy place... calm... protected... secure... peaceful... quiet... deeper and deeper... a perfect place... your muscles are so relaxed... you can barely feel your arms or legs. They're weightless... you love this feeling... floating... easy... gentle. You're less aware of the water now... and your awareness of my voice increases... my words reminds you of this perfect world... you feel safe... protected... happy ... relaxed... calm and you know... that these feelings... will remain with you... for a long time. This calm... will never fade away.

Everything in your outer awareness... everything but this beautiful place... and this beautiful calm fades... as you become so relaxed... so peaceful that my voice gets softer... and softer... and softer as you enter... the perfect state... of relaxation. You can still hear... my voice... as I guide you along through this beautiful place... the sound of my voice is in the background now... as you focus on the sights, sounds, and lovely scents all around you. Your full awareness... is focused... on this moment and the sights and sounds of this beautiful place.

As you continue to float... going deeper and deeper, deeper and deeper... into that calm... you feel your body... reach the perfect state... of relaxation... you sigh... with pleasure... at the total calm... and peace you feel. Perfectly safe... perfectly at ease... perfectly secure... perfectly protected.

[End Script]

Transition into your Hypnosis Session Script, then count-up from 10-1 slowly as indicated on the included Count-Up Script Component.

Count Down Master Hypnosis Induction

Some people really like the classic count-downs we use in our NEIH Hypnosis sessions and respond very powerfully to them. I created the following Master Hypnosis Induction which has several sequential count-downs interspersed with positive, reassuring suggestions for those individuals who want a quicker induction that still produces a full medium state of hypnosis in most individuals.

[Begin Script]

Let's begin by breathing deeply. Take a deep breath and feel the oxygen flowing through your body, relaxing you and clearing all extraneous thoughts from your mind.

As you continue to breathe deeply, imagine a small spot on the top of your head that is completely relaxed. Feel that growing sense of relaxation for a moment. Now imagine that sense of relaxation traveling down your body, through your arms, your abdomen, your legs and your feet. Feel your feet tingle just a bit as that sense of relaxation reaches them and relaxes them.

Now visualize the number 3 for a moment… hold it there… now allow yourself to imagine the number 2… hold it… and now number 1. Take a deep breath and let your eyelids and your jaw relax… allow that relaxation to move through your body… gently moving through you.

Now I'm going to count from 10 to 1. Pretend that with each number, your body becomes more relaxed and your mind becomes more open and more accessible.

[Count down slowly]

10
9
8
7
6
5
4
3
2
1

Now take a deep breath and realize that you are quickly

reaching the ideal state of relaxation. Your mind is free to soar, to imagine and to create your ideal outcome. You are entering a child like state of maximum creativity. You are a brilliant being, gifted in many ways, some as yet undiscovered and soon to be discovered. The journey into self awareness is an amazing journey of infinite possibilities. You are a genius who is writing his own life script and in this state of awareness, you are as capable as the greatest human beings among us.

Now again, I am going to count from 10 to 1. When I reach 1, you will be in a heightened state of awareness and deep relaxation. Your mind is clear and free of distractions. You are an open book waiting to write new pages for your life. Let's begin.

10
9
8
7
6

5
4
3
2
1

You are now in the perfect state of relaxation, deeply open and focused on beginning a journey of continuing discovery. There are a few thoughts I'd like to share with you:

You are born to be healthy, fit and happy. Anything less than these conditions are a lie or mis-beliefs that your mind is happy to correct. You are an infinite being, gifted in many ways. Pretend that this is true and that your current situation is a mistake that you can rewrite easily and quickly because it is. Your current situation is based on the belief that some things are fixed in time and space and that changing them is difficult. The opposite is true. Using the power of your mind to change your current situation is easy, quick and almost effortless.

[End Script]

[Transition into a Behavior Modification script component]

Metronome Master Hypnosis Induction

This is one of my favorites involving only a metronome beat for about 15-20 minutes. This will drop anyone like a rock. The script is simple. As always close your eyes or instruct your client to close his eyes. You will have recorded a metronome beat from a freeware program called Weird Metronome which you can download from cnet.com. You can use Audio Flash to record it or Audacity or a handheld high quality recorder. This induction is great for left brain dominant individuals.

Set up the metronome timer at 21 which indicates the speed of the beat. I start with this number, and incrementally decrease the beat down to 18 over a period of about 15 minutes. If you're like me, you will have a hard time staying present for 15 minutes while you are recording this metronome beat. I wandered off and handled other small projects during the recording to avoid going into a hypnotic state, then came back and adjusted the speed, etc.

When you begin to speak again after recording the metronome beat, speak very softly and slowly because it's easy to startle yourself when sound transitions into speech, so transition gently into your Hypnosis Session Script. Count yourself or client back up at the end of the session ending always with a firm Eyes Open, Wide Awake and repeat and repeat.

The Path Script Component (optional)

We've included this script component separately for ease of use. It is included as part of the NEIH Master Hypnosis Induction as well. The purpose of the script component is to introduce sights, sounds and smells, as early in the hypnotic state as possible. The more real the experience seems to you or to the person you're hypnotizing, the greater impact that it will have. Our path script component begins as soon as you or your client reaches the bottom of the stairs or have reached the ideal state of relaxation in the event that you didn't have a count-down. If you're not using stairs in an induction and still want to use the Path script component, you can just skip the round room portion.

This component is optional but allows you to integrate some Neuro-Linguistic Programming into your hypnosis session.

[Begin Script]

And as you reach the bottom of the stairs, you find yourself in a large round room with floor to ceiling windows, and you see the sunlight streaming thru the windows, warming the flagstone floor.

And up ahead you see a large oak door; you feel drawn to the door and have a sense of anticipation at the thought of moving through this doorway.

You move forward and grasp the brass door handle, and pull the door open, and as you do, you hear the hinges squeaking as you move thru the doorway into a beautiful pastoral area.

And as you look around, you see on your left a large, red barn with a shiny metal roof, and you see the sun glancing off the roof, and you are amazed at how bright the red of the barn is and as you continue to look, you see 2 black and white cows grazing contentedly in the pasture in front of the barn. As you watch them, you have a sense of their peace and contentment, and you find yourself taking on some of that peace and contentment as you walk along the path.

As you move along the path you hear the sound of the gravel crunching under your feet and you feel the cool breeze against your skin... you hear the birds in the trees above your head, you smell the flowers growing alongside the gravel path... you hear the sound of the breeze as it moves through the trees... you feel the roughness of the gravel on the path through your shoes, and you hear the sounds the cows are making as they eat the grass growing in the pasture.

As you continue to move along the path, you see a duck pond up ahead on the right, and as you look, you can see 2 ducks playing in the pond, you hear the sounds they make as they play in the water, and you can see how much fun they are having as they play in the water... as you continue to watch them, you notice to the left of the pond, a field of daisies, and you notice how the white and yellow of their flowers blend with the green of the grass, and you see how beautiful and magical this place is.

As you continue to move along the path, you hear the sounds of the birds in the trees, and you feel the breeze against your skin, and you feel the sun warming your head and your shoulders as you move along the path.

And as you move along the path, you feel the crunch of the gravel under your feet, and you hear the sounds of the birds in the trees and you feel the breeze against your skin, and you have a sense of the beauty of this magical place.

As you continue to move along the path, you notice that the path is changing to sand and as you continue to look around, you notice that you are in a beautiful beach area.

[Transition into the Self Hypnosis Session Script]

Count Up Script Component

At the end of your Behavior Modification segment of the Self Hypnosis script you're using, it's time to bring yourself or your client back to the present place and time. This is best done by relying on our tried and true Count-Up Script which can be used after the Return Path script component (original Path in reverse) or in the case that you didn't use the Path component, at the end of your Behavior Modification script component, the Count-Up Script can be used immediately.

Here's the count-up which should take about three minutes from start to finish, so proceed slowly and quietly particularly at the beginning of this script component. As you reach #7 and beyond, speak more firmly and more quickly, ending with a loudish and very firm, "eyes open, wide awake" which you will repeat several times.

[Begin Script]

#1

#2

#3 Coming back slowly…

#4 Coming back…

#5

#6 Coming back to the present moment and the present time… Coming back…

#7 Coming back, feeling fine, relaxed, refreshed, happy to be you, happy to be here, happy to be alive.

#8 Coming back to the present time and place…

#9 Coming back…

#10 Eyes open, wide awake, eyes open, wide awake, eyes open, wide awake…

[End Script]

This count-up will bring you back to the present, relaxed and refreshed. Including a count-up even if you didn't have one of the front end of the session can still be helpful for you or a client. In a hypnotic state, you are in a different reality that the one you left prior to the Hypnosis session. This count-up script allows time for a comfortable return to a fully conscious state.

Each of these Hypnosis Master Induction Scripts and Self Hypnosis Session scripts works well, so feel comfortable using the ones that appeal to you the most. Quick inductions work well for some people and not for others. I personally need a longer induction and do very well with the metronome script; the repetitive relax script or the alpha sounds scripts that we are test-driving now. These will be included in the next Hypnosis book and very possibly on the free membership website that we discuss later in the book.

CHAPTER 8
SELF HYPNOSIS SCRIPTS

In this chapter, you will find scripts for some of the most popular Hypnosis and Self Hypnosis applications. If you are looking for the Path Script component, you will find it in the Master Hypnosis Inductions chapter.

In the Master Hypnosis Inductions and these Session Scripts, you will want to use the proper cadence; a good rule of thumb is to pause slightly every 5-6 words. Using the free audio Hypnosis session on the free members website will help you to integrate the proper cadence into your sessions. More details on the free members website in the last chapter.

As you record each of these scripts, please remember to speak slowly although not quite as slowly as you will speak when using each of the Master Hypnosis Inductions which need to be spoken quite slowly.

We have left the choice of the Master Induction to you. Start each session with your chosen Master Induction, use the Path Script Component if you choose, transition into one of the Hypnosis session inductions included here and then count up to bring the client or yourself back to the present place and time. If you have used a Master Induction without a number countdown, then just repeat the same phrases we use on the count-up with or without using numbers. It's up to you. If you prefer, you can still do a count-up even if your Master Induction didn't use a countdown.

Use a quality recorder such as the ZOOM H1 or H2 or computer software and a good mic to record your sessions. When recording, keep a clock in front of you to make sure you're not speaking too quickly or too slowly or running longer than you intended. Read the induction from a computer screen when possible to avoid the noise of pages turning. Please remember to turn off your phone and cell phone and try to pick a recording time and place that is as free from interruption as possible.

Stop Smoking Now

As you continue to move along the beach, you feel the sun warming the top of your head, and you feel the sea breeze against your skin, and you hear the sounds of children's laughter. To your right, you see the ocean, and the sun as it dances on the surface of the ocean. You can hear the sounds of sea gulls as they fly above the water, and as they dive into the water, happy to be alive, just like you, and as you continue to breathe deeply filling your lungs with life-giving oxygen, the colors of the children's swimsuits catch your eye... bright reds, and lemon yellows, and sky blues. You are amazed at the remarkable beauty of this place, and you feel great... happy, healthy, glad to be alive... glad to be here, and glad to be you.

As you continue to walk along the beach, you enjoy feeling healthy and whole; you realize that this magical place has caused a complete transformation for you. You realize that you have left behind the habit that brought you here today.

You feel free, and healthy, and strong, as you move along the beach. You breathe deeply, filling your lungs with life-giving oxygen, and as you move along the beach, you notice that your clothes are a little loose, and you feel that you are releasing an extra 3-5 pounds in the process of leaving this habit behind you.

And as you continue to move along the path, you notice that there are a lot of people on the beach, but there seem to be 2 distinct groups. The group on your right is a small group, and they are more somber than the rest of the people on the beach. As you move toward them, you observe them, and you try to figure out why they seem so gloomy. As you look at them, you notice first of all, that they are sitting still, looking at the ocean and not really enjoying the beach. There are just a few of them, and as you look at them, you see that they are not interacting with each other, they are just sitting there, and then you notice that they are also smoking. And you realize as you see them, that they are not enjoying this activity, it is just something that they are doing. You sense their isolation, and you feel for them. You realize that before today, you were a lot like them, solitary and giving up a lot for a habit that wasn't really bringing you much pleasure.

As you continue to move along the beach, you notice a larger group of people ahead on your right. These people are active, and happy, playing with a beach ball while others are playing volleyball. These people are active, trim, and happy, and as you observe these people, you realize that if you had to choose the group that you now most closely resemble, it is this group of healthy, happy, active people. You breathe deeply as you walk along, and as you do, you feel your youth returning, and your breath deepening, and you feel grateful to be here, and happy to be you. You feel strong and healthy and happy as you move along the beach; someone from the active group invites you to join them in a volleyball game and you do. You are able to play well, and you feel your body growing stronger moment by moment. You thank your new friends and move along the beach path, and as you go, you marvel at your body's ability to easily and effortlessly leave behind the habit that brought you here today.

As you continue along the beach, you breathe deeply and easily. You feel your clothes growing loose on your body, as your metabolism adjusts favorably to the changes you are making. You feel your body strengthen, and as it does, your metabolism improves, in fact, your entire body responds favorably to these changes.

You realize that it is time to return the way you came, and you turn on the beach, heading back toward the path, and you wave at your new friends, still playing and laughing and expressing all the health and well-being they enjoy, and you feel grateful to be one of that group of healthy and happy people.

You realize you are completely free of the habit that brought you here today, and that you no longer desire to do anything that is harmful to your body. You realize you have been given a second chance at complete health, and you are grateful to your body for the opportunity.

As you continue to move along the path, you feel strong and free, healthy and happy, glad to be here, and glad to be you. As you continue along the path, you hear the seagulls, and the ocean waves, and you feel the sun warming your head and your shoulders, you feel the breeze against your skin, as you breathe deeply and freely, filling your lungs with life-giving oxygen. And as you continue to move along the path, you realize that we are coming closer to the pastoral area with the barn, and you look back one more time to see this beautiful place, and to remember evermore, how wonderful and alive you feel now that you are free of the challenge that brought you here today.

Lose Weight Now

As you move along the beach, you hear the sounds of the waves breaking on the shore, you hear the sounds of the sea gulls as they swoop and dive over the water's edge, and you feel the Sun warming the top of your head, and you hear the sounds of children playing, as you continue to move along the beach.

As you continue to breathe deeply, filling your lungs with life-giving oxygen, you feel lighter and lighter, and you realize that you are metabolizing food more efficiently all the time; in fact, you are digesting, assimilating, and eliminating your food easily and quickly.

You feel lighter and lighter all the time, and you have the sense of your clothing feeling a little loose on you. As you continue to walk along the path, you notice little children playing at the water's edge, laughing and having fun, as they throw a beach ball back and forth to each other. As you watch them run back and forth, you realize how much fun it is, to be able to be active again, now that you are releasing unnecessary weight.

As you continue to breathe deeply, filling your lungs with life-giving oxygen, you notice a group of people between the path and the water's edge. You see them sitting there, talking quietly to each other, and eating a lot of the foods you used to eat. And as you continue to observe them, you see that they don't look very happy, they all seem to be overweight, and as you listen to the sounds of their voices, your sense the lack of joy and happiness in that group. And you feel for them, knowing how some of them feel... left out, unattractive, and sad, you can't help feeling grateful that you have conquered the weight challenge that brought you here today, and that you are getting thinner and thinner, and feeling healthier and healthier all the time.

As you continue to walk along the beach, you smell the saltwater, and you hear the seagulls as they swoop and dive, happy to be alive, and you are happy too, and glad to be alive. You feel the sun warming your face and your shoulders, and you feel the salt-breeze as it caresses you skin, and you see the sun as it sparkles on the ocean, and you breathe deeply and feeling, enjoying the day and enjoying being you.

As you walk along the beach path, you enjoy the unfamiliar

sensation of being admired by others, and find now that you enjoy it when others look at you. You sense their approval of you, and you are grateful to realize that you deserve it and enjoy it. You feel your shyness melting away, and you feel the joy of knowing that you are doing what you can to improve your health and your looks easily and quickly. You are pleased to realize that you don't have cravings for foods that aren't good for you, and you find yourself enjoying fish, chicken, and salads. You also realize that it now takes much less food to satisfy you, and you really enjoy what you eat. You digest all the food that you eat easily and effortlessly and you assimilate and eliminate all foods perfectly. You feel your body systems speed up to accomplish your goal of reaching your perfect weight, and maintaining it easily and effortlessly. You are grateful that your body works with you to help you reach your goal. You feel your metabolism speed up, and you digest easily and effortlessly. You also assimilate and eliminate easily and quickly.

You notice as you continue to move along the beach, on the other side on the path, there is a group of very active adults...

they're playing volleyball, and throwing a Frisbee, and laughing and carrying on, and having a really fun time. These are very attractive, thin and healthy people, and you find yourself drawn to this group. As you continue to move along the beach, you notice a long table full of food... food that smells delicious. And as you continue to observe this table, you see that it is full of chicken and fish, salads, and fruit, and you realize that from this moment forward, only this healthy sort of food attracts you. You feel your mouth watering as you look at this food… you smell the food and you realize that you have never smelled anything that smelled so good.

You realize that you are really hungry, and as you continue to move slowly along the path, one of this group waves you over. You notice how slim and attractive the people in this group are, and you are aware of your own clothes growing looser. As you join this group, you realize that if you HAD to choose between this group or the group on the other side of the path, that this is the group that you would belong with. You experience such a sense of belonging and welcome from this group as they greet you and invite you to share their food. You feel so pleased to have left behind, the challenge that brought you here today. You fill a plate with good healthy food, and wonder at your food choices before today. This food is mouthwateringly good, and you eat with delight. You feel your body digesting and assimilating all the good in this food, and you feel your body begin the process of elimination as well. You are grateful that your body works so efficiently at digesting, assimilating, and eliminating all foods that you eat from this moment forward.

As you wave goodbye to your new friends, you continue along the path and see friends and family members up ahead on the left of the path. They are applauding and cheering you for having taken control of your life and your body; you feel happy and proud to be acknowledged by your friends and family for your achievement in gaining control of your weight and your life. This day is just so perfect and wonderful, and you are so glad to be able to participate in this freeing experience. You know that you are struggle-free of the challenges that brought you here today; you realize how easy it is to create everything you want in your life, starting right here and right now.

As you move along the beach, you enjoy the feeling of the sun on your face and shoulders, and you marvel at how loose your clothes feel on you. You hear the sounds of the seagulls and the roar of the waves, as they crash to the shore, and you feel the breezes caress your skin, and you decide that from this moment forward, you are free of the challenge that brought you here today, and you are free effortlessly and easily.

It's so nice here at the water's edge, and it's so nice to know that you are free of the challenge that brought you here today. Its amazing how much better you feel. Your life feels full of possibility and full of options.

As you turn on the path and begin moving back the way we came, you feel grateful and happy to be the real you, and you smile with pleasure as your friends and family applaud your successful efforts to leave behind the challenges that brought you here today. You wave goodbye to them as you continue along the path.

As you continue along the path, you hear the seagulls and the ocean waves, you feel the sun warming your head and your shoulders, you feel the breeze against your skin as you breathe deeply and freely, filling your lungs with life-giving oxygen. And as you continue to move along the path, you realize that we are coming closer to the pastoral area with the barn, and you look back one more time to see this beautiful beach and to remember evermore how wonderful and alive you feel now that you are free of the challenge that brought you here today.

General Phobias

And as you look around, you see the ocean on the left and you see children playing at the water's edge. They are playing with a large red beach ball; they're laughing and playing and as you look at them, you notice that they are wearing brightly colored bathing suits. And as you continue along the beach, you hear the sound of seagulls, and you see them swooping and diving over the ocean, you feel the warmth of the sun against your skin, and you hear the sounds of children laughing as you continue to move along the beach.

And as you continue to move along the beach, you feel the sun warming your head, you notice your clothes feel loose, and that you feel strong and confident, happy to be alive, and happy to be you as you move along the path.

And as you continue to move along the path, you smell the salt from the ocean and you hear happy beach-sounds. You are glad to be here, happy to be so strong, confident, healthy, and happy, as you move along the beach.

As you continue to move along the beach, you feel the sun warming the top of your head, and you feel the sea breeze against your skin, and you hear the sounds of children's laughter, as you move along the beach. To your right, you see the ocean, and the sun as it dances on the surface of the ocean, and you can hear the sounds of sea gulls as they fly above the water and as they dive into the water, happy to be alive just as you are. As you continue to breathe deeply filling your lungs with life-giving oxygen, you again notice the colors of the children's swimsuits; they are wearing bright reds, lemon yellows, and sky blues and violet. They are chasing a red and white striped beach ball and laughing at each other. They are having the times of their lives here on this beautiful beach. You are amazed at the remarkable beauty of this place, and you feel great - happy, healthy, glad to be alive, glad to be here, and glad to be you.

As you continue to walk along the beach, you feel yourself

becoming more and more lighthearted. There is something magical about this beach, and you take a deep breathe and realize that you are feeling more relaxed and more at ease than you have for a long time.

As you move along the beach, you see a _____ lying there on the beach. Your first impulse is to jump back and avoid it, but for some strange reason, you feel compelled to really look at it, and as you do, you notice that it is a miniature _____. And it is really cute which is kind of hard to imagine!! It looks like a toy version of a _____, and as you look at it, you feel curious and tempted to pick it up. You are amazed by your reaction to this _____, and assume that your relaxed state here at the beach has changed your normal reaction from one of dislike to one that is free of any concern. As you stand closer to it, you see that it is really cute, and you feel tempted to pick it up. As you look at it, you chide yourself for even hesitating and then just pick it up and look at it.

You find that it is really cute, with bright colors, and as you compare the reality of this small _____ with the mental/emotional image you have of this _____, you realize that your former reaction might have been a little extreme. You put the _____ in your pocket and you continue to walk along the beach, thinking about this strange situation and about life itself. You wonder how many times you have overreacted to something in your past, and decide in this moment to be free of any concerns or fears that might have limited you in the past. You realize that your new reaction to this toy _____ is more valid than the one you used to have to real _____.

You put your hand in your pocket to touch your new _____ and think how funny people are, and how funny you are in a loving and accepting way. You feel very empowered in this place and know that you can leave behind any habit or limitation that you used to embrace.

You know that you are free of the limitation that brought you here today, and you are grateful. You feel amazingly strong and in control. You feel as if you have been given a new lease on life.

As you continue to walk along the beach, you enjoy feeling healthy and whole; you suspect that this magical place has caused a complete transformation in you. You realize that you have left behind the habit that brought you here today. You feel free, and healthy, and strong, as you move along the beach. You breathe deeply, filling your lungs with life-giving oxygen and as you move along the beach you know that the process of leaving this habit behind is complete.

As you continue to move along the beach, you see some people up ahead all standing in a circle, looking at something. As you approach the group, your curiosity gets the better of you, and you go over to see what they are looking at.

You see that there is a real _____ on the ground, and you notice that your body does not register any alarm as you look at this _____. You are curious, just like everybody else and wonder how it got here. As you continue to look at the _____, you are amazed to realize that you are experiencing no sense of alarm or concern. You have clearly left behind any worry about this _____. You realize that you are free at last, and as you look at the _____ on the ground in front of you, you can't help but wonder why it ever caused you concern.

You touch the toy _____ in your pocket and you turn back and start for home. You are grateful to see how baseless the concerns were you had before and you are happy to be free of those concerns or worries you used to feel about _____. As you head for home, you smile to yourself and promise yourself that from this moment forward, you will never again be the least concerned about _____. And you realize the truth of this now.

Accelerated Healing

And as you continue to move along the beach, you feel the sun warming your head, you notice your clothes feel loose, and that you feel strong, confident, and happy to be alive and happy to be you as you move along the path.

As you continue to move along the beach, you feel a unity between yourself and all the others here at the beach. Even though you don't know most of these people, you have an absolute sense of belonging here in this place and you feel good. You feel healthy, happy, and full of joy. Your step picks up as you seem to fly along the beach. You smile at everyone you pass because you just can't contain all the joy that you feel.

As you happily move along the beach, you breathe easily and effortlessly. You are full of health, youthful and happy, enjoying being alive and happy and healthy. And as you move along the beach, you realize that you are happy just being with you and that your happiness is dependent on nothing outside of yourself. You feel free and strong and healthy as you move along the beach.

As you move along the beach, you hear the sounds of the ocean and you hear the seagulls as they swoop and dive over the water. You hear the sounds of happy children, and happy adults as they play and talk and laugh with joy - happy to be alive and happy to be here.

You feel your immune system perk up and strengthen as it begins the task of eliminating easily and effortlessly, any abnormality or irregularity that exists in your body. You feel your immune system kick into high gear and begin to scour your system of anything that does not optimize your perfect and unequivocal health. Your body can easily and effortlessly differentiate between desirable cells and undesirable cells. And as your body cleanses itself of anything that does not support your perfect health, it does so easily and with no ill effects.

You realize that your immune system is like an armed guard who is sworn to protect and defend your body. As you move along the beach, you can see up ahead a giant of a man dressed in a guard's uniform. As you get closer to him, you realize that he is a young man about 25 years of age and incredibly strong. You can see his gigantic muscles even through his uniform. He is built like a body-builder and as you look at this man, you realize that he is just like your immune system - strong and powerful and gigantic.

As you move along the beach, you are fascinated by this giant man. You've never before seen such a perfect specimen of health, power and strength. You realize that your own immune system is exactly like this man - powerful and young and inexhaustible. You feel your immune system growing stronger as you allow yourself to see the truth of this situation. You have been blessed with a tremendously powerful immune system that grows stronger every day in every way so that it can protect you from any infirmity.

You feel confident and safe as you walk along the beach,

grateful to your body for providing you with such a powerful protector. And you realize from this moment forward, that your immune system is more than capable of protecting you from any foreign invader or abnormality that may exist in your body. You realize that your immune system is skilled at detecting which cells need to be eliminated and which are cells to be maintained. Your body's immune system protects you daily from any imbalance or infirmity.

As you move along the beach, you realize that it is time for you to return to the path. And as you turn to walk in the direction toward home, you are grateful to be protected so thoroughly by your immune system. You enjoy the power of accelerated healing and know that your body is capable of protecting you and healing you effortlessly. You realize this and feel a sense of gratitude toward your body as you continue to move along the beach.

As you move along the beach toward home, you hear the sounds of the ocean, you hear the seagulls as they swoop and dive over the water, and you hear the sounds of happy children's laughter and happy adults as they play, talk and laugh with joy - happy to be alive, happy to be here and happy to be you.

Stress Release

As you continue to move along the beach, you feel the sun warming the top of your head, you feel the sea breeze against your skin, and you hear the sounds of children's laughter as you move along the beach. To your right you see the ocean and the sun as it dances on the surface of the water, you can hear the sounds of sea gulls as they fly above the water and as they dive into the water, happy to be alive just like you. As you continue to breathe deeply filling your lungs with life-giving oxygen, the colors of the children's swimsuits catch your eye - bright reds, lemon yellows, and sky blues.

You are amazed at the remarkable beauty of this place, and you feel great - happy, healthy, glad to be alive, glad to be here, and glad to be you.

You feel any sense of tension in your body melt away, feeling free and young and full of life, certain of a happy outcome for this and every day. As you move along the beach you feel yourself relaxing, breathing deeply, feeling good, feeling fine with a light heart and a happy mind. As you move along the beach, you see other people walking and talking along the beach, you see others laying on beach towels enjoying the beautiful day, and you feel a part of this happy scene. You have a sense of belonging here, you feel accepted and valued by the others as well as by yourself. You realize that from this moment forward, you have a clearer view of whom you are, and how well you fit into the world. You let out a deep sigh and with that sigh you release any stored tension from your body.

You realize that you are now free of any sense of concern you might have carried around with you before today. You feel as if someone has given you a crystal ball that allows you to see all of the outcomes ahead for you, and you see that all is well. You take a deep breath and as you do, you feel your body bathing in the extra oxygen you are providing with your full and deep breathing. You realize that you are completely free of any sense of anxiety or concern. You feel your heart open with happiness, as you leave any concerns or worries behind.

As you continue to breathe deeply, you feel yourself becoming more and more relaxed moment by moment. You realize that this level of relaxation is now yours, without any effort on your part.

As you continue to move along the beach, you see a beautiful seashell lying there in front of you. As you pick it up to admire it, you realize that this seashell can be your reminder of this perfect sense of relaxation you are enjoying today. From this moment forward, the word "seashell" causes your body to return to this perfect sense of relaxation. And as you look at the seashell, you feel a deeper sense of relaxation moving over you. Then you say the word "seashell" and you feel an even deeper sense of relaxation move over your body. And with this, you feel a true and abiding sense of the perfection of your world and your place in the world. You realize that you are free forever more of any concerns or worries that might have occupied your mind before this day.

As you continue to move along the beach, you see so many seashells on the beach, and just for fun, you say seashell, seashell, seashell, and each time that you do, you feel your body respond positively by relaxing more and more to the word that has become a signal to your body to relax.

And as you move along the beach, you breathe deeply and you realize how healing it is to breathe deeply. You feel your body respond to all of the oxygen that you are taking in. You decide that from this moment forward, you breathe deeply and fully, filling your body with life-giving oxygen.

As you continue to walk along the beach, you smell the salty air and you hear the seagulls as they swoop and dive, happy to be alive and you feel happy too and glad to be alive, just like the seagulls. You feel the sun warming your face and your shoulders, you feel the salt-breeze as it caresses you skin, you see the sun as it sparkles on the ocean, and you breathe deeply and freely, enjoying the day and enjoying being you.

It's so nice here at the water's edge, and it's so nice to know that you are free of the challenge that brought you here today. It is amazing how much better you feel. Your life feels full of possibility and full of options.

As you turn around on the path moving back the way we came, you feel grateful and happy to be the real you, free of your emotional armoring, and you smile with pleasure as your friends and family again applauds your successful efforts to leave behind the challenge that brought you here today. You wave goodbye to them as you continue along the path.

As you continue along the path, you hear the seagulls and the ocean waves, you feel the sun warming your head and your shoulders, and you feel the breeze against your skin as you breathe deeply and freely filling your lungs with life-giving oxygen. As you continue to move along the path, you realize that we are coming closer to the pastoral area with the barn. You look back one more time to see this beautiful beach and to remember evermore how wonderful and alive you feel now that you are free of the challenge that brought you here today and how grateful you feel for this experience.

Happy Relationships

You are a truly happy person who enjoys other people. You are skillful and friendly at work and everyone is aware of that. You receive a lot of positive attention and reinforcement from others, and you deserve it. It is great to know that you can handle whatever life sends your way. You are a strong, confident, happy and successful person.

You walk proudly with your head held high. You know that you are a good person and a good employee or boss. You are cooperative with others and since you know your own value, the success of others doesn't threaten you. You rejoice at everyone's success.

You realize that others like you and recognize your abilities. You accept the friendship of others gratefully, and know that it is given honestly to you. Even though you are a very remarkable person, you are modest in your dealings with others.

As you walk along the beach, you smile to yourself and you remember a phrase from long ago and you agree with it – "To have a good friend, you need to be a good friend", and that's your motto. You are a good friend to others. You are a generous and kind person, and you express these qualities to others freely. You are a good friend to others and you are always willing to lend a helping hand. Your friends willingly reciprocate.

You are a truly friendly person who enjoys being liked and being involved with lots of people. You are fascinated by people, so you find their stories interesting and you offer support and advice when people ask for it. You are grateful to have been given a strong and loving heart and you share your heartfelt concern for those people in your life. You can be relaxed in your life because you know that whatever comes along, you have lots of friends to support you.

You truly enjoy peaceful and cooperative relationships with others. You are able to relate pleasantly with your spouse, your parents, your siblings and all children. You deserve respect and consideration from others and you get it as well as give it. You truly enjoy happy relationships in your life.

As you turn around on the path moving back the way we came, you feel grateful and happy to be the real you, free of your emotional armoring, and you smile with pleasure as your friends and family again applauds your successful efforts to leave behind the challenge that brought you here today. You wave goodbye to them as you continue along the path.

As you continue along the path, you hear the seagulls and the ocean waves, you feel the sun warming your head and your shoulders, and you feel the breeze against your skin as you breathe deeply and freely filling your lungs with life-giving oxygen. As you continue to move along the path, you realize that we are coming closer to the pastoral area with the barn. You look back one more time to see this beautiful beach and to remember evermore how wonderful and alive you feel now that you are free of the challenge that brought you here today and how grateful you feel for this experience.

Supreme Self Esteem

And as you continue to move along the beach, you feel the sun warming your head, you notice that your clothes feel loose, and that you feel strong, and confident, happy to be alive, and happy to be you, as you move along the path. And as you continue to move along the path, you smell the salt from the ocean, you hear happy beach-sounds, and you are glad to be here and happy to be so strong, confident, healthy as you move along the beach.

To your right, you see the ocean and the sun as it dances on the surface of the waves, and you can hear the sounds of sea gulls as they swoop and dive above the water full of life just like you. As you continue to breathe deeply filling your lungs with life-giving oxygen, the colors of the children's swimsuits catch your eye; they are wearing suits of bright reds, and lemon yellows, and sky blues, and you are amazed at the remarkable beauty of this place. You feel great; happy, healthy, glad to be alive, glad to be here, and glad to be you. As you continue to move along the beach path, you notice that there are a lot of people on the beach and you feel happy to be one of them. You notice people glance your way and in the glances you see approval and in some, admiration. It makes you happy to experience this kind of acceptance from others. You smile with the pleasure of it all.

As you continue to move along the beach, you feel your spirits soar; you feel good and attractive and worthy of achieving and receiving what you desire. You feel younger and lighter, attractive and desirable, and you like these feelings. You chuckle to yourself as you walk along the beach because you suddenly realize the truth of your situation; the truth is that you are lovable and worthy of love. You expect to be valued by others and you are. It's time that you begin to value yourself, too.

As you walk along the beach, you are becoming aware that others are looking at you. You are very aware that they are looking at you not with criticism, but with open admiration.

You find that you are now comfortable with the attentions of others, in fact, you are enjoying the attention!

As you continue to walk along the beach, you notice that your posture has improved; you are holding your head high, and moving in a strong and confident way. You feel an awakening in you of a true and complete awareness of your goodness, your kindness to others and your value as a human being. You are grateful to finally see the truth about yourself. You decide from this moment forward to always allow yourself to see the truth about your value and you are glad to be able to do so.

As you continue to move along the beach, you notice a group of people up ahead on the left hand side of the beach. They are playing volleyball and you really wish you could be playing volleyball, too. You enjoy watching the friendly competition among the players and you really feel that you could add something to the game. One of the men playing closest to you sees you and invites you to play. You grin at him, accept and begin to play the game. You find that you can play well and with confidence, and you laugh out loud at the sheer pleasure of moving your body in play. You are able to play well and you feel your body growing stronger and stronger, moment by moment. You feel strong and powerful and you know that this is the truth of who you are, in play and out of play. The game ends and you wave goodbye, really grateful for having had the opportunity to play. You decide to take time to play more often.

As you continue to move along the beach, you continue to be aware of the admiration of others, and you rejoice in your comfort with that attention. You realize that you were always worthy of that attention, and you are grateful now to be comfortable receiving that attention from others. You are a remarkable and valuable person, who is deserving of all the best that the world has to offer.

You know that you are now free from the limitations that brought you here today and you are grateful for that. You feel amazingly strong and confident and in control of your life. In fact, you feel as if you have been given a new lease on life.

It's so nice and peaceful here at the water's edge; it's even nicer to feel comfortable with yourself and to have a truer understanding of who you really are. It is amazing how much better you feel, and how much better your life feels now-full of possibilities and options.

As you turn on the path, moving back the way we came, you feel grateful and happy to be able to express the real you to others. You are grateful to have gained the understanding that you are a person of true value, and you feel happy that you have allowed yourself to perceive the truth about you.

You are also pleased to find how comfortable you are in the company of others. All in all, this has been a wonderful day and you look forward to a lifetime of wonderful days!

As you walk along the beach, you have a sense of contentment and happiness and you feel this contentment filling you and you are so glad!

Breathe Easy

As you continue to move along the beach, you feel happy and healthy, full of life, full of health, and you are looking forward to a wonderful day at the beach.

As you move along the beach, you feel the sun warming the top of your head and your shoulders and your face, and you have the sense that this is one of those perfect days that we all occasionally experience with perfect weather, perfect place, and perfect you.

As you move along the beach, you hear the sounds of the ocean, the seagulls as they swoop and dive over the water, and you hear the sounds of happy children and happy adults as they play on the beach, talking and laughing with joy - happy to be alive and happy to be here.

As you continue to move along the beach, you feel your endocrine system tuning up, strengthening and supporting more fully all of your body's needs. You feel strong and sharp as you move along the beach. You have tremendous mental clarity as you reflect on what has come before, and what you would like to create in your life at this time.

As you move along the beach path, you feel your strong skeletal system; you know your bones are strong and growing stronger, and you feel your cardiovascular system becoming stronger and healthier.

You feel your immune system strengthen, as it begins the task of eliminating easily and effortlessly any abnormality or irregularity that exists in your body. You feel your immune system kick into high gear and begin to scour your system of anything that does not optimize your perfect and unequivocal health. Your body can easily and effortlessly differentiate between desirable cells and undesirable cells. As your body cleanses itself of anything that does not support your perfect health, it does so easily and with no ill effects.

As you move along the beach, you notice that there are a lot of people here today, many who appear to be around your age. A few are running a race on the beach, and you feel the desire to be able to breathe well enough to be able to run again. Instead of accepting limited breath, you allow yourself to imagine yourself breathing freely and strongly and as you do so, you realize that you can at least walk vigorously, and so you begin to do so. As you do, you feel your body respond to the walking with gratitude and strength. Your body loves to move and walking briskly is filling your lungs and body with life-giving oxygen and you feel great.

As you watch the others, you notice that they are strong and fast; their bodies seem to be in perfect condition. As a group they are slim and trim and so full of life. You hear their laughter as the winner jumps up in the air in joy, as the others clap her on the back. As you move along the beach, you find yourself re-evaluating this stage of your life. You had expected to feel your body weakening as you aged and yet today you feel it strengthening. You are surprised and pleased to feel stronger and stronger by the moment, and you realize that you can have more and more of this feeling of health and vitality.

And as you look around and see these strong, active people, you rejoice in your body's ability to transform itself so powerfully and easily. As you stride along the beach, you feel strong, you breathe easily and deeply, and you realize that you can take in all the air that exists in the world if you want it. You feel your lungs expand at this staggering thought and you breathe fully and deeply. Breathing is again completely effortless and as the oxygen fills your lungs, you feel powerful and free to walk or run or do whatever you want. As you hold tight to these healthy feelings, you look ahead to a time when you are older and you see a healthy and active older version of you. You realize from this moment forward, that perfect health and easy breathing are yours for the taking.

As you continue to breathe deeply, walking strongly and purposefully down the beach, you feel healthy, young and strong, and grateful to your body for its renewal. As you smile to yourself for just feeling so good, you see others smile back to you in return and you realize you are wearing your happiness on your face for all to see. And so you smile again.

As you continue to move along the beach, you realize that it is time to return back the way we came, and you are grateful and happy to be here, breathing like a 12 year old - happy, strong, healthy and you.
[Return and Count-Up]

Finding True Love

As you continue to move along the beach, you feel the sun warming your head, you notice your clothes feel loose, and that you feel strong, confident, happy to be alive, and happy to be you as you move along the path.

As you continue to move along the Path, you smell the salt

from the ocean, you hear happy beach sounds, and you are glad to be here and happy to feel so strong, confident, healthy, and happy, as you move along the beach.

As you continue to move along the beach, you are amazed at the beauty of this place. This magical place seems to call to you as you walk along the beach and you feel the sun warm the top of your head, you see more children playing happily at the water's edge, and you hear the happy sounds of adults at play.

You feel at one with the people on the beach and you are glad to be here and to be you. You realize you are a person who is destined to love deeply and well, and you look forward to finding your own true love.

You realize that there are many good people in the world and that finding your perfect mate is an easy task. Now that you are ready to meet your dreamboat, you know that you will soon.

As you move along the beach, you look around at the people and you see many of these people interacting lovingly with each other. You see men and women walking along holding hands, and girls and boys as well. As you notice their loving glances and happy laughter, your reaction is one of pleasure at the happiness you are observing. You are surprised to realize that you never really allowed yourself to see how completely surrounded by love that we all are. You have a true sense that love is out there just for the asking. And as you look at the people on the beach, you feel your heart open and welcome you own mate to find you or visa versa.

As you move along the beach, you hear the sounds of the ocean, you hear the seagulls as they swoop and dive over the water, and you hear the sounds of happy children and happy adults as they play and talk and laugh with you. You wave and share a happy smile with all, as you are feeling very happy to be alive and happy to be here. You feel so much a part of this place, these people and this day. You are grateful to be a part of the loving interactions all around you. You know that all you need to do to attract your perfect mate is to continue to remain open to him/her; the laws of attraction will guide you two to each other. As you continue to move along the beach, you decide in this moment to be completely open to love. You feel so happy and so free and so sure of the love that you desire. You trust the Universe to deliver the perfect person to you in the shortest possible time.

As you move along the beach, you allow yourself to imagine who your perfect person is, how he/she looks and the personal traits he/she possesses. As you contemplate these things, you feel at peace - not pressured or discouraged but full of hope and life. You have that happy feeling you get right before something wonderful happens.

As you continue to breathe deeply, you allow yourself to acknowledge your true value and to realize how completely deserving of love that you are. You acknowledge how kind and caring you are and how willing you are to give as well as receive in a loving relationship. You feel your heart open even more as you allow yourself to imagine the wonderful feeling of being completely loved and of loving completely.

You realize that from this moment forward you are free of any cares or concerns about past relationships that may have been disappointing. You realize that you have left the past behind and you are ready and able to move forward into the perfect relationship.

As you move along the beach, you decide to sit at the water's edge and to contemplate the person you are seeking. Take just a moment, to allow yourself to envision your perfect mate, to see his/her face, and to hear his/her voice. Allow yourself to look into his/her eyes, and to invite him/her to come to you now or shortly. Ask him his name. If the image of his face is not clear, do not be concerned.

Concentrate on communicating with his soul and on calling his name, inviting him to join you in your life in the here and now. Imagine that there are many strands of gold threads in your solar plexus area. Allow one of them to leave your body, moving through the universe and connecting with one of the gold threads in the solar plexus of your perfect mate.

Allow your gold thread to connect with his gold thread. Invite his soul to shorten the thread day by day until you and he are face to face. Let him know how much you miss him and want him. Allow your heart's desire to move through time and space and to communicate with your perfect mate. Allow yourself to contemplate this process and allow this process to occur naturally and esthetically.

I will be quiet for a moment. When I begin to speak again, my voice will not alarm you.

(PAUSE for about 3 minutes. Begin to speak quietly)

You realize that it is time to return to our walk along the beach. You feel changed and blessed by your experiences today. You feel completely connected to your mate and you look forward to meeting him/her. You realize that from this moment forward, you can return to the beach (in your mind) and to the communication you have shared with your Beloved by simply finding a quiet spot, closing your eyes, and saying the word BEACH. In that moment, you are instantly transported to this time and space and can again enjoy communing with your Beloved.

As you continue to move along the beach, you feel the sun warming your head and heart, and you feel so blessed to have spent time in this wonderful place. You are confident that your perfect Mate is on his/her way to you and that you will instantly recognize him/her when you meet face to face. You feel as if you have been sprinkled with gold dust, and you are happy to be here and happy to be you.

[Return and Count-up.]

Avoiding Cancer

As you continue to move along the beach, you feel happy and healthy, full of life, full of health, and you are looking forward to a wonderful day at the beach.

As you move along the beach, you feel the sun warming the top of your head, your shoulders, and your face; you have the sense that this is one of those perfect days that we all experience occasionally. Perfect weather, perfect place, and perfect you.

As you happily move along the beach, you breathe easily and effortlessly. You are full of health, youthful and happy, enjoying being alive, happy and healthy. As you move along the beach, you realize that you are happy just being with you, and that your happiness is dependent on nothing outside of you. You feel free and strong and healthy as you move along the beach.

As you move along the beach, you hear the sounds of the ocean, you hear the seagulls as they swoop and dive over the water, and you hear the sounds of happy children, and happy adults as they play, talk and laugh with joy - happy to be alive and happy to be here.

And as you continue to move along the beach, you feel a

unity between yourself and all the others here at the beach. Even though you don't know most of these people, you have an absolute sense of belonging here in this place. You just feel good. You feel healthy, happy, and full of joy. Your step picks up as you seem to fly along the beach. You smile at everyone you pass because you just can't contain all the joy that you feel.

As you move along the beach, you have a sense of anticipation. You know something wonderful is coming and you look forward to finding out what it might be.

As you continue to move along the beach, you see someone up ahead who looks familiar to you. At this distance, you really can't be sure who it is but you have a sense that it is a man and that he is a very good man.

As you continue to move along the beach, you see that a crowd is forming around this man. You hear the excited talk that surrounds his appearance and as you get closer, you realize why he looks so familiar. He looks exactly like

Einstein; he's dressed in white, and you realize that everyone else is probably thinking the same thing you are. You know that it can't be Einstein, but he sure looks like him.

And now you notice a line forming in front of this Einstein look-a-like. It looks like he has some sort of needle-like instrument in his hand. You get in line, so you can find out what is happening here, and you watch as this gentleman smiles at each person and gives them something that looks a little like a shot, but you don't think that it is. As you continue to get closer, you see that everyone laughs as the man puts this cylindrical metallic object against each person's arm. You are so curious about what is going on, even though it all seems a little strange, you feel very excited and happy to be here in this place and in this line.

And now it is your turn, and the man in white asks you to roll up your sleeve. You ask him what this is for, and he explains that he is giving everyone an inoculation against cancer. Anyone who has cancer will recover immediately with no discomfort and anyone who doesn't have it, will never get it. You ask him if it hurts, and he says that it feels wonderful!! Looking around at the happy faces, you know that this must be true.

After a moment's hesitation you hold out your arm and as he presses the metallic cylindrical object against your arm, you feel a warm sweet feeling coursing through your body. You can feel it as it enters your body; it feels like liquid light as it flies through your bloodstream, cleansing and healing, and through your bones and organs, cleansing and healing. You laugh out loud just as the others did as you realize that from this moment forward, you are permanently free of cancer.

You cannot get it, and if you had it a moment ago, you no longer do now.

You realize how free you are, free of the worry of cancer, and free to live a healthy and happy life. You trust absolutely that this is true. You have the sense of being part of a shared miracle and feel grateful for the experience.

As you move past the man in white, you look around and see the joy you feel mirrored in the faces of the others.

You feel full of joy, strength, health, and peace. As you look back at this wonderful man, you realize how happy you are.

As you turn to walk back the way you came, you see that the line is getting longer and longer, as others discover the wonderful man in white. You hear the laughter of the newly healed and you share their joy.

As you move along the beach returning home, you hear the seagulls, you hear and smell the salty ocean and you feel the sun on your head like a benediction. You realize what an invaluable gift you have been given today.

As you move along the beach, you sense your growing health and well-being, as you breathe deeply and freely - happy to be alive, happy to be here, happy to be you.

[Transition back to the Count-Up]

Cardiac Health

As you continue to move along the beach, you feel happy and healthy, full of life, full of health, and you are looking forward to a wonderful day at the beach.

As you move along the beach, you feel the sun warming the top of your head, your shoulders, and your face; you have the sense that this is another one of those perfect days we all have experienced. Perfect weather, perfect place, and perfect you.

As you move along the beach, you hear the sounds of the ocean, the seagulls as they swoop and dive over the water, and you hear the sounds of happy children and adults as they play, and talk and laugh here on the beach.

As you continue to move along the beach, you feel your endocrine system tuning up, strengthening and supporting more fully all of your body's needs. You feel strong and sharp as you move along the beach. You have tremendous mental clarity as you reflect on what has come before and what you would like to create in your life at this time.

As you move along the beach path, you feel your strong skeletal system; your bones are strong and growing stronger and you also feel your cardiovascular system becoming stronger and healthier. You feel any irregularities in your cardiovascular system gently and easily correct themselves.

As you continue to move along the beach, you feel your respiration become stronger; you breathe deeply and easily as you enjoy the fragrances found here on the beach. You also enjoy the warmth of the sun on your head and your shoulders, and you enjoy the smell of the salt air and food being grilled on the beach.

You hear the sounds of children playing on the beach; you see the running and tumbling and hear their laughter mingle with the sounds of grown-ups talking and chuckling, enjoying the day.

You feel good and healthy and fortunate to be in this beautiful place. You vow to allow yourself to enjoy every moment of your great life and to take more time for you.

As you continue to move along the beach, you feel strong, healthy, and you feel your cardiovascular system becoming younger and stronger as you move along the beach. You have a strong sense that this is true. You also have a joyful sense of the long and healthy life ahead of you. You are grateful for your strong and healthy body.

Up ahead you notice a sign on the right hand side of the beach by the water's edge. You move toward it so you can read it and see that it says to read the information enclosed in the little box attached to the signpost. You take out the literature and start to read, and as you do, you notice that everyone on the beach seems to be reading these brochures. Now you are really curious, so you start to read.

And here is the essence of what the brochure says: everyone on the beach today can request perfect health, and if in that request there is truth, then perfect health will be granted. As you look around you, you notice that everyone seems to be a little dazed by the information in the brochure.

The instructions are to sit along the water's edge and to silently articulate your desire for perfect health; at the moment that your desire is 100% genuine, your body will be rejuvenated.

You look around to see if others are going to follow the instructions; you decide in this moment that you are going to sit at the water's edge and do as instructed, even if you are the only one doing so. And you do.

As you sit there, allowing yourself to silently articulate your total desire for complete physical rejuvenation, you feel a strange thing start to happen. You feel the slightest change in your body; you feel different somehow and suddenly you are filled with the most radiant joy. You can't accurately describe this new feeling, but your body feels as if every cell in your body is experiencing total ecstasy. This amazing feeling continues for a few moments, and then it is gone, replaced with a sense of quiet joy.

You look around and notice that a few people have joined you at the water's edge, and they too seem to be having some sort of inner experience much like yours. The others look like you feel - happy, healthy, and reborn in some way. You have a sense of knowing that your entire body has been rejuvenated. You know that your entire cardiovascular system is now that of a young person, and you are so glad. You know that from this moment forward, you can expect to experience perfect health and you vow in this moment to make healthy decisions for your body and to strive to maintain this level of perfect health with good food and regular exercise.

You feel like dancing down the beach but you restrain yourself in an effort to maintain just a modicum of dignity. You feel so alive and so grateful to be given a chance to begin again.

You know that your body is now much younger than your chronological age, and you are thrilled to have your strong healthy body back.

As you turn on the beach heading back the way we came, you are grateful and pleased with your day at the beach, and even though you don't understand the miracle that you and others here experienced today, you accept it with joy.

[Return and Count Up]

Defeating Alcoholism

And as you look around you see the ocean on the left and you see children playing at the water's edge. They are playing with a large red beach ball; they're laughing and playing and having the time of their young lives. As you look at them, you notice that they are wearing colorful bathing suits of red, sky blue, orange and lime green. And as you continue to walk along the beach, you hear the sounds of seagulls which you see swooping and diving over the ocean. You feel the warmth of the sun on your skin, you hear the sounds of children laughing and the sounds of the ocean as you continue to move along the beach.

And as you continue to move along the beach, you feel the sun warming your head, you notice your clothes feel loose, and that you feel strong, confident, happy to be alive, and happy to be you as you move along the path.

And as you continue to move along the beach, you smell the

salt from the ocean, you hear happy beach sounds, you are glad to be here and happy to be so strong, confident, and healthy as you move along the beach.

And as you look around you see the ocean on the left and you again notice the children playing at the water's edge; they are playing with a large red beach ball. They're laughing and playing and as you look at them, you have an absolute sense of their joy at being alive.

And as you continue to move along the beach, you notice your clothes feel loose, and that you feel strong, and confident, happy to be alive, and happy to be you, as you move along the path.

As you continue to move along the beach, you feel happy and whole; you realize that this magical place has caused a complete transformation in you. You realize that you have left behind the habit that brought you here today. You feel free, healthy and strong as you move along the beach. You breathe deeply, filling your lungs with life giving oxygen and as you move along the beach, you sense a healthy appetite for food returning to you. You look around to find a place to buy some food and as you do, you smell a barbeque close at hand. You smell the aroma of food being grilled on the beach, that ambrosial smell of hotdogs and charcoal grills, and salt, and the sea. You realize that your desire for food is in many ways a desire for life, and a healthy one at that. And you are glad.

You notice as you continue to move along the beach that on the other side of the path, there is a group of people cooking food. They seem like friendly people, and the food smells amazing. You had no idea you were so hungry. You notice that they have a table of food with barbequed chicken, fish, salads and fruit, and you realize that your appetite has returned with a vengeance. You feel your mouth watering as you look at this food. When you smell the food they're cooking, you realize that you have never smelled anything that smelled so good. One member of the group waves you over and invites you to join the group. You feel a real sense of belonging and welcome from this group as they greet you and invite you to share their food; you also feel valued and lucky to be invited by strangers to join them. You fill your plate with salads and fish, and you are amazed at the wonderful taste of this healthy food. You feel your body digesting and assimilating all the good in this food, and you feel your body begin the process of elimination as well. You are grateful your body works so efficiently. You realize from this moment forward, you have no desire for anything which does not support your body's health. You also realize that in the process of enjoying this food and beverage, you do not feel that you are missing anything. All your desires around the consumption of food and beverages have been satisfied. You feel full of hope and delight that you do not need or desire anything to drink with your food other than water, iced tea, or a soda. In fact you realize that from this moment forward that you are free of the desire for any beverages that do not serve your highest good. You liver is strengthened and healthy, and you are able to digest this delicious food easily and effortlessly.

As you wave goodbye to your new friends, you continue

along the path and you breathe deeply and easily as you move along the beach path. You are amazed at how well you feel and how healthy you are. You are looking forward to increasing health and wellbeing. You feel happy and proud for your achievement in gaining control over the habit that brought you here today. You feel like kicking up your heels in celebration of having regained control of your life. This day is just so perfect and wonderful and you are so grateful to be free of the habit that brought you here today. You realize now how easy it is to create everything you want in your life.

You feel any sense of tension in your body melt away, feeling free and young and full of life, certain of a happy outcome for this and every day. As you move along the beach, you feel yourself relaxing, breathing deeply, feeling good, feeling fine with a light heart and a happy mind. As you move along the beach, you see other people walking and talking along the beach, and you see others lying on beach towels, enjoying the beautiful day, and you feel like you are a part of this happy scene. You have a sense of belonging here, you feel accepted and valued by others, as well as by yourself. You realize from this moment forward, you have a clearer sense of who you are, and how well you fit into the world. You let out a deep sigh, and with the sigh, you release any stored tension from your body.

You realize that you are now free from any sense of concern you have carried around with you before today. You feel as if someone has given you a crystal ball that allows you to see your future, and you see that all is well. You take a deep breath, and as you do, you feel your body bathing in the extra oxygen you are providing for it by breathing deeply and completely. You feel your heart open with happiness, as you leave any worries or concerns behind you and return back the way we came.

[Transition back to the Count-Up]

Menopausal Support

As you continue to move along the beach, you feel happy and healthy, full of life and health, and you are looking forward to a wonderful day at the beach.

As you move along the beach, you feel the sun warming the top of your head, your shoulders and your face. You have the sense that this is one of those perfect days we all have experienced - perfect weather, perfect place, and perfect you.

As you move along the beach, you hear the sounds of the ocean, you hear the seagulls as they play over the water, and you hear the sounds of happy children and adults as they play, talk and laugh with joy- happy to be alive and happy to be here.

As you continue to move along the beach, you feel your endocrine system tuning up, strengthening and supporting more fully all of your body's needs. You feel strong and healthy as you move along the beach. You experience remarkable mental clarity as you reflect on what has come before and what you would now like to create in your life.

As you move along the beach path, you feel that your bones are strong and growing stronger, and you feel your cardiovascular system becoming stronger and healthier. You know that this time of life is natural and your body supports you perfectly during this period of hormonal transition.

You feel your immune system perk up and strengthen, as it begins the task of eliminating easily and effortlessly any abnormality or irregularity that exists in your body. You feel your immune system kick into high gear and begin to scour your system of anything that does not optimize your perfect and unequivocal health. Your body can easily and effortlessly differentiate between desirable cells and undesirable cells and does so at this time. And as your body cleanses itself of anything that does not support your perfect health, it does so easily and with no ill effects.

And as you move along the beach, you notice a lot of women, many who appear to be about your chronological age. A few are running a race on the beach, and you stop a moment to admire these women. They are strong and fast; their bodies appear to be in perfect condition. They are slim and trim and happy, admirably so. You hear their laughter as the winner jumps up in the air in joy and the others clap her on the back. As you move along the beach, you find yourself re-evaluating this time in your life. You had expected to feel a weakening in your body and yet you feel your body strengthening. You are surprised and pleased to feel stronger and stronger every day. And as you look around and see these strong, active women, you rejoice in your body's ability to transform itself so powerfully and easily.

As you move along the path, you decide to join this group of strong, active 50ish women. They welcome you. You take one aside and ask her how it is that she is so strong and active; she whispers a secret in your ear, and you laugh to hear how simple it is to be just like she and the other women.

This wonderful secret empowers you and moves through your mind changing you physically and mentally. You feel your body growing stronger and leaner in this moment. You realize that from this moment forward, your body grows stronger and leaner, your bones grow stronger and denser, your mental clarity increases, and your sense of well-being grows moment by moment.

As you continue to move along the path you feel full of joy, strong, healthy and happy. You are happy to be alive, happy to be here, and happy to be you. You feel blessed to have received this wonderful benediction, as you feel your body glow and prosper moment by moment. As you look at these wonderful women, you realize that you are free of the concerns that you brought here to the beach today. Your body supports your desire for growing strength and provides it for you. You feel your body integrate the changes that you desire and you are glad. You feel your bones strengthen, you feel your heart relax and heal the hurts from the past, you feel your mind becoming clearer, you feel your memory sharpen, and you feel your endocrine system powerfully protecting your body during this change by easily and efficiently regulating the hormones that support this process. Your body releases excess weight and optimizes all of your systems. All of this is done effortlessly, instantly and easily.

As you move along the beach, you hear the seagulls, you hear and smell the ocean, and you feel the sun on your head like a benediction. You feel a sense of gratitude for the gift you have been given by these wonderful women on the beach.

As you move along the beach, you sense your growing health and well-being, as you breathe deeply and freely - happy to be alive, happy to be here, happy to be you.

As you move along the beach, you realize that it is time to return. You are grateful to be protected so thoroughly by your endocrine system. You realize this and feel a sense of gratitude toward your body as you permanently release any concerns you felt about this natural and normal hormonal transition.

[Transition Back]

Easy Pregnancy & Birth

As you continue to move along the beach, you feel happy and healthy, full of life and brimming with good health. You are looking forward to a wonderful day at the beach.

As you move along the beach, you feel the sun warming the top of your head, your shoulders, and your face. You sense that this is one of those perfect days that we all have experienced occasionally. Perfect weather, perfect place, and perfect you.

As you move along the beach, you hear the sounds of the ocean, you hear the seagulls as they swoop and dive over the water, and you hear the sounds of happy children and adults as they play, and talk and laugh with joy- happy to be alive and happy to be here.

As you continue to move along the beach, you feel your endocrine system tuning up, strengthening and supporting more fully all of your body's needs. You feel strong and powerful, healthy and happy as you move along the beach. You find that your digestive system works well; that you are able to eat whatever you want with no distress. The food you eat satisfies you and goes down easily.

As you move along the beach path, you feel your bones are growing stronger moment by moment and day by day. You feel your cardiovascular system becoming stronger and healthier. You know that this time of life is natural and your body supports you and your baby perfectly. You know that your body is the perfect home for your baby's growth and development. It is easy for you to eat sensibly, to exercise as you much as you want, and to maintain ideal body weight for you and the baby.

As you move along the beach, you feel your pelvic area strengthening in preparation for the birth of your child and you feel your body creating the perfect incubator for your child's development. You feel your abdominal muscles growing stronger and more flexible. You are amazed at how incredibly well you feel at this wonderful time of your life. As you move along the beach, you see a large group of pregnant women on the left side of the path. As you observe these women who seem to be sitting in a group waiting for a speaker. They look like an audience, and you go over there and sit down too. As you look around, these women appear to be at varying stages of pregnancy. They all look healthy and happy. You feel a real bonding with these women and feel a true sense of belonging. The woman next to you smiles at you and just as you begin to ask her what's going on here, a woman walks to the front of the group. She is beautiful in an exotic way and she is wearing Native American clothing. She raises her arms in a benediction for the group and you feel a surge of energy move through you. You feel a tingling throughout your body that is very pleasant.

This woman speaks quietly about the power of women, how strongly we are built for this blessed work of bringing children into the world, and how powerful each of us is. She explains that she has been gifted with a power to support women in this blessed work, and that she will be placing her hands on each of our heads for a few moments. She explains that in those few moments our bodies will be strengthened and our systems stepped up to support even more perfectly our pregnancy and the birth of the baby. The women in the audience began raising their hands and offering testimonials to this woman's work. They report a pregnancy saved, a baby miraculously turned moments before a C-section was necessary, an older mother delivering a healthy child easily and effortlessly against all odds.

You feel the love these women feel for this Native American woman called Na-oh-ha who had helped so many of them. You are thrilled to have happened upon this group and you wait patiently for Na-oh-ha to get to you. You watch as she patiently and loving puts her hands on each woman, and you feel the sense of well-being and happiness that fills the group.

And finally she reaches you and puts her hands gently on your head as she murmurs words that you cannot hear. You feel a sense of warmth move through your body, and a sense of quickening as if the baby feels it too. A lovely liquid feeling moves through you as you surrender to the experience, marveling at the way your body feels. As she moves on to the next woman, you allow yourself to try to measure the changes that have occurred in your body. You feel stronger and more flexible, fearless and protected. You feel loved completely and absolutely.

As Na-oh-ha finishes with the last woman, she sits and we form a circle around her. She explains that each of our babies is healthy and perfectly formed, that each of us is programmed for an easy birth, and a quick and easy healing after the birth. She asks that we bow our heads and sit quietly in a group and thank our God for this blessing and allow ourselves to rejoice in this wonderful news.

We do and when we raise our heads we find she is gone. You feel a momentary sense of alarm, but the woman next to you touches your hand and explains that she always leaves in this way. The blessing is complete and your easy pregnancy and birth are assured. This woman hugs you, and then gets up to go. And you do as well.

As you start back up the beach, the way that you came, you feel blessed and strong, healthy and somehow changed. You feel better than you ever have before and you know that an easy pregnancy and birth are yours. You hope that you will find these women again, so that you can celebrate the joy of life, the power of your body, and the power of that woman's loving goodness.

As you move along the beach, you hear the seagulls, you hear and smell the ocean, and you feel the sun on your head like a benediction. You realize what an invaluable gift you have been given.

As you move along the beach, you sense your growing health and well-being as you breathe deeply and freely - happy to be alive, happy to be here, happy to be you.
[Transition Back]

Supreme Self Confidence

As you continue to move along the beach, you know that you are a competent person. You are skillful at your work and everyone notices this. You receive a lot of positive attention and reinforcement from others and you deserve it. It is great to know that you can handle whatever life sends your way. You are a strong, confident and successful person.

You walk proudly with your head held high. You know that you are a good person and a good employee/boss. You realize that others are attracted to you and that most people seem to recognize your abilities. Your accept praise gratefully and you know that it is honestly given to you. Even though you are a remarkable person, you are modest in dealing with others. You accept praise as your due without becoming self-absorbed and cocky.

As you walk along the beach, you smile to yourself as you remember a phase from long ago and you agree with it; the

phrase goes, "If you've got it, don't flaunt it."
You know that you can successfully tackle any task that is given to you. You have accomplished a lot in your life through hard work and intelligence and you do stop occasionally to acknowledge your efforts. You also know that you can achieve any goal you set for yourself.

You are a truly remarkable person who enjoys supreme self-confidence. You are grateful to have been given a strong and logical mind as well as a strong creative side. You can relax in your life because you know that whatever comes along, you are fully capable of handling it.

As you turn toward home, you smile at the happy changes you feel occurring inside you.
[Transition Back]

Diabetes Support

As you continue to move along the beach, you feel happy, healthy, and full of life. You are looking forward to a wonderful day at the beach.

As you move along the beach, you feel the sun warming the top of your head, your shoulders, and your face, and you have the sense that this is one of those rare perfect days- perfect weather, perfect places, and perfect you.

As you happily move along the beach, you breathe easily and effortlessly. You are full of health, youthful and happy, and enjoying being alive. And as you move along the beach, you realize that you are happy just being with you, and that your happiness is dependent on nothing outside of you. You feel free and strong and healthy as you move along the beach.

As you move along the beach, you hear the sounds of the ocean, the seagulls as they swoop and dive over the water, and you hear the sounds of happy children and adults as they play, talk and laugh with joy - happy to be alive and happy to be here.

And as you continue to move along the beach, you feel a sense of unity between yourself and all the others here at the beach. Even though you don't know most of these people, you have an absolute sense of belonging here in this place, and you feel good. You feel healthy, happy, and full of joy. Your step picks up as you seem to fly along the beach. You smile at everyone you pass because you just can't contain all the joy that you feel.

You feel your immune system perk up and strengthen as it begins the task of eliminating easily and effortlessly any abnormality or irregularity that exists in your body. You feel your immune system kick into high gear and begin to scour your system of anything that does not optimize your perfect and unequivocal health. Your body can easily and effortlessly differentiate between desirable cells and undesirable cells. And as your body cleanses itself of anything that does not support your perfect health, it does so easily and with no ill effects on your body. You realize that your mind can make corrections to your body's functioning with no ill effects. You feel strong and free, and you celebrate that feeling.

As you continue to move along the beach, you feel a change occurring on your left side under your rib cage. You feel an energizing that starts small, and then expands. As the energy expands, you feel your body growing even stronger and you feel your blood sugar levels optimizing, balancing and maintaining the perfect level. As your body makes these changes you feel very blessed and grateful to your body for choosing perfect health for you. You realize that your body normally chooses to protect you by maintaining existing conditions, and you also realize that when necessary your body welcomes new instructions from you, to truly maintain perfect health and balance. You feel your blood sugar levels adjusting to provide you with perfect health and balance.

You feel your pancreas calming, functioning perfectly and you feel your liver and gallbladder responding positively to these happy adjustments. You realize that your body is capable of functioning absolutely flawlessly and it is doing so right now at your instruction. You feel strong and healthy and free of the imbalance that brought you here today. You trust that your pancreas is healing and balancing, returning your blood sugar levels to normal levels and maintaining that normalcy.

You realize from this moment forward that your body makes all the adjustments necessary to insure your perfect health and well-being. You give your body permission to make corrections that assure your perfect health.

As you continue to move along the beach, you breathe deeply and feel the strength increasing in your body moment by moment. You feel healthy, happy and grateful to be here today.

As you turn to head toward home, you feel strong, and young and healthy and happy. You move along the beach with power, grateful to your body for the changes you have made.

[Transition Back]

Strengthen Your Immune System

As you continue to move along the beach, you feel happy and healthy, full of life, full of health, and you are looking forward to a wonderful day at the beach.

As you move along the beach, you feel the sun warming the top of your head, your shoulders, and your face. You sense that this is going to be a great day so you look forward to its unfolding - perfect weather, perfect place, and perfect you.

As you happily move along the beach, you breathe easily and effortlessly. You are full of health, youthful and happy, enjoying being alive. As you move along the beach, you realize that you are happy being on your own and that your happiness is dependent on nothing outside of you. You feel free, strong and healthy as you move along the beach.

As you move along the beach, you hear the sounds of the ocean, you hear the seagulls as they swoop and dive over the water, and you hear the sounds of happy children and adults as they enjoy their day at the beach - happy to be alive and happy to be here.

And as you continue to move along the beach, you feel a unity between yourself and all the others here at the beach. Even though you don't know most of these people, you have an absolute sense of belonging here in this place, and you feel good. You feel healthy, happy, and full of joy. Your step picks up as you walk quickly along the beach. You smile at everyone you pass, because you just can't contain all the joy that you feel.

You feel your immune system perk up and strengthen, as it begins the task of eliminating easily and effortlessly any abnormality or irregularity that exists in your body. You feel your immune system kick into high gear and begin to scour your system of anything that does not work toward optimizing your perfect and unequivocal health. Your body can easily and effortlessly differentiate between desirable cells and undesirable cells. And as your body cleanses itself of anything that does not support your perfect health, it does so easily and with no ill effects.

You realize that your immune system is like an armored guard protecting your body. As you move along the beach, you can see up ahead of you, a giant of a man dressed in a guard's uniform. As you get closer to him, you realize that he is a young man, about 25, and incredibility strong. You can see his gigantic muscles even through his uniform. He is built like a body builder, and as you look at this giant, you realize that he is just like your immune system - strong and powerful and gigantic!

As you move along the beach, you are fascinated by this giant. You realize that your own immune system is like this man - powerful, young and inexhaustible. You feel your immune system growing stronger as you allow yourself to see the truth of these words. You have been blessed with a tremendously powerful immune system that grows stronger every day, so that it can protect you from any infirmity. You feel confident and safe as you walk along the beach, grateful to your body for providing you with such a powerful protector. And you realize from this moment forward, that your immune system is more than capable of protecting you from any foreign invader, or any abnormality that may exist in your body. You realize that your immune system is skilled at detecting which are cells to be eliminated and which are cells to be maintained. Your body's immune system protects you daily from infirmity.

As you move along the beach, you realize that it is time to return to the Path. And as you turn to walk in that direction toward home, you are grateful to be protected so thoroughly by your healthy and powerful immune system. You realize this and feel a sense of gratitude toward your body for providing you with such perfect protection.
[Transition Back]

Past Life Regression

I recommend always following a script with a PLR because the process is pretty standard. When we are mucking around in someone's subconscious memories, it's great to have on hand the anchor that the script represents.

[Please use one of the Master Hypnosis Inductions to induce the appropriate state and then proceed with the following script.]

I'm going to count downward from 10 to 1. Allow yourself to relax fully and completely. Don't concern yourself with the process, just trust that you will receive the benefits you desire.

[Slowly 10, 9, 8, 7, 6, 5, 4, 3, 2 and 1] And now you can just close your eyes, and you can keep them closed. And I will explain what that was for; it was just to relax your eyelids. And right now, in your eyelids there is probably a feeling of

relaxation... and you find this a pleasant sensation.
[If the client does not seem to be at the proper stage of relaxation- fidgety, or rapid respiration, or nervous eyelid blinking, go thru the 10-1 down the stairs again slowly, or you may vary it to going down a spiraling staircase as you count down the numbers.]

I will count rapidly now--- 9, 8, 7, 6, 5, 4, 3, 2 and 1. You are now at your own natural level of relaxation. And from this level you may move to any of level with complete awareness, and you can function at will. You are completely in control at every level of mind, and you can accept or reject anything that is given here to you today.

You are in control. There is something you long to discover, and so our journey begins.

My voice is your guide, and as we progress, you discover that you can listen to my voice, and also deal with other things at the same time. You are a person of many abilities, so my voice does not distract you as we continue along our journey. You can relax...you don't need to try to do anything...your subconscious is here and can hear every word that I am saying.

As you take a deep breath, you feel yourself drifting; you feel less and less need to listen closely to my voice. In your own time, today, tomorrow, next week, your subconscious mind will reveal what it has uncovered to you in a dream, or at a moment of consciousness, but at the perfect moment in the perfect way. You will be given memories of other times and places, memories you thought were gone, only to be discovered again. And with these newly found memories comes new insights, new growth, new understanding. And stored deep in your subconscious mind are wonderful memories. Your subconscious mind can access and recall these memories and bring them back with you later.

So, by looking deeply into your mind, you can see your soul's vision and hear the voices of experiences captured far in the past. Your subconscious mind can access these memories and bring them back to you later.

Can you remember a time in your life when you really felt safe?

[PAUSE]

And you may begin going back to around the time you were 18 years old -- choosing a pleasant and happy memory of about the time you were 18 years old. You will find that this is very easy for you to do -- choosing one specific memory or event -- and just simply focusing on it, looking at the people around you and then looking at yourself.

I will be quiet and give you plenty of time to simply enjoy this event. You may hear voices or you may simply feel the presence of people. You may see as clearly as in a movie, or the images may be vague. You may see these things in your mind's eye -- you may hear voices and sounds from this time whispered in your ear. You may only sense the memory. It doesn't matter. It doesn't really matter in what way you perceive your memories. You are about 18 years old now. What is happening??

[LONG PAUSE]

Now you may continue going back to about the time you were 5 or 6 years old. Again choosing a pleasant happy memory, an impression, or a specific experience from about the time you were 6 years old. Focus on this experience; look at this memory clearly. See what you were wearing, sense or feel the people around you. Look and listen to the information. Allow yourself to watch these experiences as if you were sitting in the seats of a movie theater. You are not re-experiencing this; you are just observing the 6 year old you. You are 6 years old now.

[LONG PAUSE]

Now continue going back to about the time you were 4, and then 3, and then 2, and now 1. And keep going back to the time of your birth. And going even beyond that to that warm and safe place from which we all come. You are where nothing can harm you; you are perfectly safe, perfectly secure, perfectly protected, perfectly at peace. You feel loved and completely warm and protected. This is the time of your beginning, of growing, a time of movement, and a time of preparation. This is a very good time, and you can travel beyond this time and place as well.

You are now going into the Rose Mist that feels so soft and safe. And the Rose Mist surrounds you and protects you. You are very safe and comfortable here; the Rose Mist is a time of inner peace, tranquility, quiet movement, gentle sounds, and gentle light. You like it here very much because you can experience real peace and serenity, real joy here. You are so comfortable here, and yet a part of you longs for more - movement, life; and this longing grows within you until it becomes stronger and stronger. And this desire allows you to look outward, and as you look outward, you see a light, as if you were looking down a long tunnel. The light is good. You feel drawn toward the Light and you feel yourself moving toward the light. You are traveling along the pathway of the soul. The light enters you thru the top of your head and fills you with light. The light heals you... protects you... surrounds you... as you feel life energy flowing thru your being; you feel a quickening in you which is life. You realize that you now exist in separation from the

Mist and other beings and that you are in incarnate form. This realization comes over you and you want to understand it. You allow yourself to look down towards your feet and you notice what you are wearing on your feet. Plant your feet and your consciousness firmly on the ground and notice what you are wearing on your feet. Don't allow yourself to analyze the experience, but just glance down and mentally record what you are wearing on your feet, and what you sense or feel about this moment. You may wish to say this aloud. What are you wearing on your feet?

[PAUSE]

And now you can continue looking up your body, at what you may have on the bottom half of your body. Feel the texture... determine whether it is fabric or metal or animal skin... see the colors of your garment. Continue looking up the body now, and look at what you have on the top half of your body. Now allow yourself to glimpse the entire body and I will be quiet for a moment. What are you wearing? What is covering all or part of your body? What sort of body do you have?

[PAUSE]

Notice any jewelry you may be wearing, and allow yourself to observe whether you are wearing anything on your head and whether you have any jewelry on your hands. Focus on allowing yourself to take in as much information as possible. Allow yourself to see clearly as you peacefully and gently explore the scene around you. Process this information and if possible, take a mental picture of it. Look at your entire body, and I will be quiet for a moment. Are you wearing jewelry? Are you wearing adornments of any sort?

[PAUSE]

Now, with your mind's eye, look around slowly to see where you are situated and make a note of it. Are there trees, mountains, sand, the ocean, a lake, a stream, or buildings?? Look around and record what you see. And again I will be quiet while you make a full turn around yourself, looking in all directions, and making a note of the important things you see. Mentally record as much of this information as you can so that you can examine it later. What do you see? Is it a familiar scene or is it some place entirely new to you?

[PAUSE]

And now, you may look for other people. Who is around you... how are they dressed... are you in a group of men, or women, or are you alone?? If you are alone, you may look to another time when there are people around you. Make a note of these people, and record the information mentally so you may access it at a later time. If there are people, do they look familiar? Is there someone special nearby... someone with whom you have a special relationship or a special fondness? Look around you... perhaps there is a child or an adult who is dear to you. Are you part of a community or are you one of only a few other people present? Mentally record these feelings and impressions. If you listen closely, you may even hear names being mentioned. Who is there with you?

[PAUSE]

And now you may look for a vehicle of transportation... something you may have ridden on or in. Are there carriages, or wagons, or beasts of burden? Is there someone there who is currently using a means of transportation? Make a note of the means of transportation. Do you see any forms of conveyance? Is this a place of commerce, activity and many forms of conveyance or it is a quiet, less active place? Answer these questions either out loud or in your mind so that you can review this information later.

[PAUSE]

And at this time, you may feel hungry. What is it that you eat when you are hungry? Can you smell the food cooking? Are you able to taste it?? Are there smells of food or cooking? Is there a store or place to buy food items near you? If so, what does it look like? Record your impressions. What do you see and smell?

[PAUSE]

And now, if your listen quietly, you may hear friends call out your name to you. What is it? What are you doing... what is your work or your job. Do you seem to have an occupation or something that occupies your time? If you don't work, are you a student? If so, what are you learning?

[PAUSE]

And as you look around yourself for clues, do you get an impression of where you are? What land is this? What is this land called... what is the name of this place? Are you in a forest, a desert, a mountain top or valley? Or are you in a city with public transportation, lots of people and lots of activity? Perhaps you can sense what century or what year this is. Do you know what year this is? Ask someone who is close to you or look for a newspaper or printed calendar?

[PAUSE]

And now you may move to a major event in your life, a time that has important meaning for you, and focus on what is happening. This may be a big event or a small event; it doesn't matter as long as it has significance for you. Can you recollect or return to the moment of a major event in your life?

[PAUSE]

And what is happening next? What moments follow the event of importance to you?
[PAUSE]

And what is happening now... what are you doing??

[PAUSE]

And now in a detached way, as a bystander, look at the time of your death in this incarnation. Death is simply the next stage of life. What events have led up to your death? How did you die? Allow yourself to witness these events without feeling them in a painful way. What do you experience after your death? Look at the death experience and ask to assimilate its messages.

[PAUSE]

What is the reason or purpose for this life? What are the lessons for your Soul? Was it a happy life? What made you the happiest in this life? Was anything left uncompleted in this life? If so, you may return to complete it. Take your time; I will wait for you.

[LONG PAUSE]

And now that you have received all this information, bring it all together into a vivid symbol or a series of symbols, and wrap it up in something familiar to you, so that you can bring all this information back with you. Encode this information in your mind in a way that will make it easy to access. Allow yourself to encapsulate this experience and trust that you will be able to access the information that has value for your present life and that you will release the information that has no value for your present life.

Most important of all, mentally look into your own eyes and

the eyes of those around you, and those you have loved, and that special person. Look into the eyes of everyone you saw and send love from your eyes to their eyes. And as you bless them, forgive them, and send them your love, they begin to fade. And as they begin to fade, let them go. Release them, bless them, forgive them, and let them go as they bless and forgive you. Let the veil drop slowly. Allow the curtain to slowly close, and allow a full healing of this life and of this time.

[PAUSE]

And as you slowly begin coming back, traveling thru time and space, you can bring back with you all that was positive, interesting, and significant to you. Simply release and close the door on information or impressions that are not necessary for your soul growth at this time. Bring back only that which has value for you. You will retain in you conscious mind only what is helpful and beneficial to you at this time.

Now you are coming back to and thru the light, once again

traveling on the avenue of the soul, where all things are known to you thru that warm and safe place where nothing can harm your returning thru the levels of the mind to the clear recall of your own mind, and bringing back the information that you have recorded. Slowly now, slowly now, coming back to the present life to _____ (date) in _____ (city, state). Plant your feet firmly in the present... step fully and happily into your present life.

And in a little while, when you are fully awake, you will feel just wonderful. You will feel better than before. You will be wide awake, clear-headed, and happy and you will feel relaxed, refreshed, happy to be alive and happy to be you. Your subconscious mind always protects you and knows what is best for you.

[Slowly count back up. Take your time.]
I will count from 1 to 9. At the count of 9, you can open your eyes, be wide awake, feeling great, feeling fine, happy to be alive and happy to be awake. I will count now.

#1 - coming back very slowly now; #2 - coming back very slowly now; #3 - coming up now; #4 - feel your energy returning to you; #5 - feeling totally normal and perfectly fine; #6 - feeling re-energized; #7 - coming up to your full potential; #8 - fully awake and fully aware of your surroundings; #9 - feeling revitalized; #10 - wide-awake-open your eyes now-wide-awake.

[After you are out of your session, take notes about this past life regression. Number and date the session notes in case you decide to do other past life regressions.]

CHAPTER 9
WRITING YOUR OWN SCRIPTS

Even though we've provided you with a variety of Hypnosis Session scripts, you will find one day soon that there's an application you'd like to work on that's not included in this book. Yikes!

Don't worry; the transition from using canned scripts to your own custom scripts is easy.

First, define the exact application that you'd like to work on. By define, I mean delineate it in every way you can. Pretend you're your own client and interview yourself about this application. Here is some of the information you will want to collect.

If it's a habit you'd like to break:

When did it start?

Why did it start?
How did it start?
Why do you want to stop this habit?
What's the pay-off for stopping?
How will your continuing affect other people?
How will your stopping affect others?
Who else will gain the most from your stopping?

This information is the source material for the suggestions you will create for your session. As you interview yourself and write down your answers, you are helping yourself to understand the situation more fully. In a conscious state, you are reviewing what motivates this habit and what motivates stopping this habit. This is powerful pre-hypnotic programming, so take your time with this process.

The first 3 questions serve the purpose of clarifying the breadth and depth of the habit. It takes about 18 days to make a habit, so if your habit has been operating for 20 years you will need to give yourself a bit of time to change the behavior. Without hypnosis, it takes 38 days to stop a habit.

With hypnosis, the process is much quicker but the actual length of time depends on you, the script you create, your feelings about Hypnosis, and your desire to change the habit. Hypnosis doesn't turn people into robots. You still exist in free will, so you have the choice of directing your free will toward stopping a habit or continuing one. It's up to you and the decision you make definitely affects the outcome of your Hypnosis sessions.

For suggestion creation, you will use the answers to the last 5 questions to create your custom suggestions and to populate the behavior modification section landscape with virtual observers and supporters. See the stop smoking hypnosis session script for an example of this.

Let's use stop smoking as an example hypnosis application. In any session, it's good to have custom suggestions and some standard suggestions. Good standard suggestions are available in any of the included Hypnosis session scripts. Here are a few:

-You breathe easily and deeply.

-You feel your clothes getting looser as you walk along the beach.

-You feel younger and healthier than you have in years.

These are positive, present tense, short suggestions that would work well in many different Hypnosis sessions. When creating your own suggestions, be sure to keep them simple, present tense, and positive. One of the ways to stay in the positive tense when you want to suggest a future outcome is to use this one:

"From this moment forward" suggests a future outcome while staying in the present tense.

Okay, back to creating your custom suggestions. Using the answer, "I want to stop smoking so that I won't get lung cancer." you might create this suggestion:

"*Your health is assured when you take positive actions to*

stay healthy."

For the answer, "I want to stop smoking so my clothes don't smell bad", you might create these suggestions:

"Your clothing and body scent is fresh and clean." "You love the way your clothes smell."

For the answer, "I want to stop smoking because my boyfriend John doesn't want to kiss me now that I smoke", you might create the suggestions:

"John finds you totally appealing. He loves the way you smell."

"John is so grateful that you take his needs into consideration."

"John tells everyone how thoughtful you are."

I want to discuss briefly how the above answer led me to

create these suggestions. We want to create short, present tense, positive suggestions. We also want to create a utopian situation in the session that the client's mind or your mind will find irresistible. John is rejecting our pretend client on a very emotional level by not kissing her. The suggestions I created indicate the opposite of the current situation. They are actually pay-off suggestions that reward the client or self in advance for making the behavior change that is desired. In addition, creating suggestions that jump to the reward phase takes the focus off what is being "lost" to what is being gained. Also, operating in the reward phase strongly suggests that the change has already been made. In the Behavior Modification portion of the script, we are operating within the belief framework that the desired change has already occurred.

These simple suggestions shown above actually address the last four interview questions mentioned above. You could build upon these suggestions and expand to an imagined situation in which John begins to make behavioral changes that would please the client. You could have John suggest a weekly date night. Creating suggestions that add value to the success of the process for yourself or a client is the key to great Hypnosis sessions. And since it's all in your mind and the client's anyway, the sky is the limit. Suggest amazing and wonderful things and then watch them show up in your life or your client's life.

If you choose to work with a friend or family member, you will find that the best way to create great suggestions for someone else is to pretend for a moment that you *are* this other person. Create suggestions that would work for that pretend "you." Once you realize how much easier this technique makes the suggestion creation process, you will become more comfortable with it. I feel that this is the best way to find the perfect language choices and content, and to create the perfect suggestions for any other person you might choose to work with.

CHAPTER 10
SETTING THE STAGE FOR SUCCESS

How do you maximize the likelihood of your success with Self Hypnosis? Here's how.

If you're using an included Master Induction and Session Script, review both until you are really familiar with them.

If you are ready to create your own Hypnosis Session Script, explore the specifics of your application as much as possible by self examination using the how, why, when, and pay-off questions to make either a behavioral or attitudinal change. Write down the answers to these questions on a large paper tablet just as if you were interviewing someone else.

After you're sure that you've examined the application as completely as possible, create at least 7 custom suggestions. Make sure that your suggestions are relatively short, simple, present tense, and positive. Then add 3-5 standard suggestions you will find in the Hypnosis Session Scripts that you feel will add to the quality of the Hypnosis session.

Have a good quality recorder on hand and ideally a lapel mic. I can recommend a good quality recorder that doesn't need an extra microphone (I use this one for my sessions) and 2 microphones in case you will be using a recorder that needs a mic:

Olympus ME-15 lapel microphone is available at Amazon.com for about $23.

Audio-Technica ATR3350 lapel microphone is also available at Amazon.com for around the same price.

Zoom H1 or H2 Digital Recorder with an integrated microphone is available at Amazon.com for $125.and $142.

The quality of the recording is critical to your success. If you end up listening to a static-y Hypnosis session because you bought an inexpensive recorder, you may find that the static makes it hard for you to go into the appropriate state of Hypnosis. Buying a good quality recorder will pay for itself over and over again. If you decide to work with friends or family, you will definitely want to give them quality recordings to reinforce your session. I have never regretted buying good quality AV equipment but I have regretted saving a few dollars on the wrong equipment. If it's not convenient right now to buy a Zoom or comparable quality recorder now, use Audacity (free software for your computer) and buy a nice quality lapel microphone. To find this software, Google Audacity and you will be taken to a Source Forge download site. Audacity is good software, not as easy to use as a Zoom recorder, but if you use a good mic, it will produce a nice quality recording for you.

Record your session in a place where you can control as much as possible, the ambient noises around you like the furnace, central AC unit, the refrigerator and so on. Outside noises such as airplanes, trains, subways, buses, lawn mowers and the highway can also blemish your recording so organize around these sounds also.

Pick the time of day you record your session to minimize predictable noises. A day or so before recording a session, take time to become aware of all the sounds around you and figure out how many of the sounds you can control. You will want your recording to be as good as you can make it. Pick a location in your house and a time of day that is as free as possible from predictable noise.

Be sure to turn off your cell phone and the landline phone if you have one. Also turn off your Skype, if you use it.

Decide ahead of time where you will sit during your recording. A recliner is ideal because it's comfortable and many of us associate relaxation with being in a recliner. Make sure you have water on hand in case your mouth gets dry. Know where the pause button is on the recorder and how to use it in case you need to cough or some loud unexpected noise starts up close to the recording spot.

Have a written script preferably on a laptop or tablet to avoid rustling pages as you move through the script. Drink lots of water before starting your recording, time your script in advance so you know how long it should take to complete it at your ideal cadence, and have a clock right in front of you so that you can keep track of the time. Get comfortable and record. Your session should be between about 25 minutes and 45 minutes using the Master Hypnosis Inductions included in this book and the Hypnosis Session Inductions. The Quick Inductions will take about 25 minutes and using the NEIH Master Hypnosis Induction and one of the Hypnosis Session Inductions will take closer to 45 minutes.

I would recommend that you consider starting your Self-Hypnosis work using Hypnosis scripts that are included in this book. That will allow you as soon as you want to experience Self Hypnosis, learning how your body responds to Hypnosis and taking any pressure off you to create a Hypnosis Session Script at the start. Record several sessions using different Master Hypnosis Inductions to see which type or combination you prefer. When you are ready to create your own sessions, you will have gained a lot of information from using the included inductions and session scripts.

Once you have a complete session recorded, make a commitment to take 30 or 45 minutes a day to use your Self Hypnosis session. Listen to your session with headphones daily for two weeks or so. It will relax you, and that quiet time can be healing in ways that you might not expect. Continue with that first session as long as you choose. There's no such thing as too much Self Hypnosis.

When you are working or driving, don't play your session because you won't want to enter a hypnotic state in either of those situations. I know that seems self evident, but you would be surprised how many people think that using a Self Hypnosis CD while driving is a good idea. It's not.

For times like driving or working, you can always use positive affirmations to reinforce your sessions. Positive affirmations are really just the suggestion portion of a Self Hypnosis session or any other positive statements that appeal to you. Running positive affirmations in your head quiets any self talk you're dealing with and focuses your mind on positive outcomes. Write down on a 3x5 card 10 statements that you'd like to see active in your life. These statements don't have to be about the purpose of your Self Hypnosis sessions. Any positive affirmation is good; they don't take the place of Self Hypnosis but they certainly can't hurt. Like Hypnosis suggestions, affirmations should be positive, short and present tense.

Speaking of positive, limiting your contact as much as possible to positive people will speed any quantum upgrades you're hoping to accomplish in your life. If you deal with negative people while you are choosing to be positive, you will end up spending a lot of energy counteracting the effects of their negativity. Energy you could be spending creating more positivity. As you become happier and more positive, you will attract more positive people naturally so this process will take care of itself eventually.

I'll share a Silva Method technique I've been using since 1984. When someone says something to me that is negative or something that I don't want in my head, I say cancel-cancel to myself and picture in my mind a giant red X through what I just heard. My brain has learned that this means, "don't take in this information." When too much negativity is being spoken to me or I'm hearing it on TV or spoken by an individual, I have been known to say it out loud. You have the option of choosing to be the sole person who programs your mind, and if you decide that's what you want, mentally canceling that which you don't want, works for me and millions of other Silva grads. Try it out and see what you think.

One last thing. Many of our students over the years have asked this question, so in case you're wondering whether you can combine 2 or more Hypnosis applications in one Self Hypnosis session, we don't recommend it. I think you'll find that focusing on one Hypnosis application at a time will work best for you.

Creating your own Self Hypnosis sessions and your own scripts is a powerful first step to creating a better life for you and for anyone who deals with you regularly. You will be amazed at how easy it is to create quantum changes in the quality of you life. Facilitating these changes can require as little as 30 minutes a day. Amazing!

CHAPTER 11
ADJUSTING TO THE NEW YOU

Change is good, right? You've been working hard to create change and you've achieved it! You've arrived at the new you, but the "old" you left footprints in the sand all around your life. The new you may feel a bit foreign to you, but to others it likely feels as if the person they've known forever has been abducted by aliens and this new "pretend" you has been left on earth to take his/her place. Okay, that's a bit of an exaggeration, but there is some truth here.

Throughout the years you were "old" you, you've had numerous interactions with other people. And with family and close friends, even more. In the course of those years, you have taught people who you are. They have learned what to expect from you, how much you will put up with, and how to get their way with you. We all teach those around us how to manage us. In fact, we teach them well.

Individuals who feel less than they really are often put up with a lot more than they should, in terms of behavior they accept from other people. Those around us learn what to expect from us, but when we change and become thinner, more confident, more relaxed, and more powerful, the way we interact with others changes. We expect more and frequently put up with less than we used to. As you might imagine, the "new" you is often a big surprise to those around you. You're different, more confident, and less easy to manage. Yes, you look better and are happier and more fun, but interacting with you can be a lot more work than it used to be.

This adjustment period with friends, family and acquaintances can be managed more easily if you expect it and prepare for it. People are funny. They can want you to be thinner or more relaxed and yet when you accomplish these goals, they can feel threatened. I think of it this way. When you've known someone for a long time, he or she has "learned" you; in some ways you're like part of the wallpaper. You're a constant and thus require a lot less attention than you did at the beginning of your interactions.

When you change your mind and/or your body, it will probably require some work for others to re-learn you. Many people don't like it when the "wallpaper" suddenly changes, requiring additional effort relearning this new version of you. Some people don't like when anything changes, so when a person in their sphere changes all the rules because he/she has experienced a huge personal growth spurt, the transition isn't always seamless.

Can you stop others from reacting to the changes in you? No. Many will celebrate your great success, a few will resent it and a few will find it very inconvenient. This is natural and it will pass. Be who you are, celebrate your own success, be kind and patient as others adjust to the new you, but don't give up any ground. Achieving personal growth always comes at a price. To transition from "old" you to new you required a lot of effort and commitment on your part. You've made it and done what many never will do. It is cause for celebration and if everyone isn't celebrating right away trust that they will when they get used to the new you. Some relationships may not make the transition, but that's okay. There's an expression that has always given me a lot of comfort as I've transitioned through my own growth stages. No one can take away what's truly yours and conversely you can't hold onto what's not. Relationships that fail to make the transition would have failed at some point anyway. And honestly, if you're in a relationship with someone who values his/her own convenience above your happiness; is that a relationship you want to continue?

This is all the good news. You've set goals for yourself and accomplished them which is the bottom line. And forewarned is forearmed. Expect the best of everyone but don't come unglued if everyone doesn't embrace the new you right off the bat. Those people in your life who are keepers will ride the wave of your personal growth cycles and celebrate your successes with you, as they stay by your side learning this new and improved version of you!

CHAPTER 12
ASSURING YOUR SUCCESS

If someone told you that you could have anything you want if you were willing to invest 45 minutes a day, would you do it? Would you take the chance?

Because, dear reader, that is where you are now. You have the tools you need to create a better life for yourself and those you care about. And your dollar investment can be as little as $40 including the cost of this book and a microphone. Amazing. Or you can continue on the path that led you to buy this book in search of a better life.

If you decide to move forward and use Self Hypnosis to tackle your wish list, then I have a few suggestions for you that will help you to succeed.

Be patient. A friend told me once that transformation occurs in an instant after a lifetime of trying. She was joking although I suspect she believed it. My version of that saying is that transformation can occur almost simultaneously if you are willing to focus your genius on the changes that you choose.

That said I still believe that patience is one of the keys to achieving your highest outcome. Be kind to yourself and be patient with yourself. Take one day at a time and give yourself the gift of your undivided attention for 45 minutes daily while you enjoy your Self Hypnosis session. Make that session a priority and organize around it whenever possible.

Be kind. As you change, the people in your life will need to change too, to accommodate the changes in you. Be kind to them and to yourself. Change is almost always good because change promotes growth, but change isn't always easy. Kindness can ease the way for everyone who is in your circle of influence.

Be positive. Once you start on a Self Hypnosis program for yourself or someone else, assume that it's already a done deal. Assume that the changes have already occurred and that you're just waiting for those changes to show up in present reality.

Don't second guess yourself. You have what you need to make amazing changes in your life. Move forward day by day, using Self Hypnosis to create a better life. Keep your eye on the prize and do the work. You will find that you feel happier, more rested, sleep better and just feel better overall. Trust that you're on the right path and continue to move forward on that path. What do you have to lose?

Enjoy the process. You may not realize this, but you are engaging in a magical process. Let's face it. You relax deeply, listen to 8 or 9 suggestions while you are in a relaxed state and your life improves. If it's not magical, I don't know what is.

If this is the first time that you've used Hypnosis to improve your life, then you have some wonderful surprises ahead. Take your time and allow yourself to be aware of the big and small changes that are taking place in your mind and in your life.

Keep a journal. I know journaling is in style, but that's not why I'm suggesting it. If you were going to see a professional Hypnotherapist, he would be keeping a file of your sessions and the progress you're making. In the case of Self Hypnosis, it's up to you to keep some notes on the changes you're making. You're important and so is this process. Keeping track of your thoughts and the changes you make in your life will have a lot of value for you as you look back after creating your desired changes. It will make you happy to have a record of your experiences and your thoughts about the process while the process was occurring. Once you've achieved your goals, you can't go back and recapture this fleeting information. Taking an extra 5 minutes to note changes and thoughts every couple of days during this process will reward you grandly.

Try different Master Hypnosis Inductions. It's normal to keep doing what you're doing but it is fun to try something new. When you find your favorite Master Induction, use it again and again because repetitious use will entrain your brain. However, until you try other inductions, you won't know if you have found the best one for you. Try one of the other Master Hypnosis Inductions just for fun.

Have one new session ahead. As you experience your Self Hypnosis sessions, you will change and so will your life. It's great to be ready for either another application or to move on to the next session in a series of sessions that you've planned. Try to have one new recorded Hypnosis session ahead so that you can progress as soon as you feel ready to do so.

Look ahead. If you are like many users of Self Hypnosis, you may fall in love with the process and want to work in this field. Your practice with Self Hypnosis will stand you in good stead as you will develop confidence in the process. If you decide that you want to train as a Certified Clinical Hypnotherapist, please consider NEIH as your training source. As a reader of QSH and a member of the Quantum

Self Hypnosis members website, you will be eligible for a training discount. Please feel free to visit the NEIH website at http://neih.com for information on our training programs.

Join the QSH free members website. First of all, it's free, and joining will give you the FREE audio Hypnosis session that will help you to anchor in the cadence used in Hypnosis. The session will also give you confidence in using Hypnosis and help you to integrate and easily access all that you are learning as you read this book.

As a member, you will also be able to connect with others, enjoy training bonuses, and more. You can find the members website at http://quantumselfhypnosis.com.

And last but not least, thank you for reading this book. Writing it was a labor of love and a source of real pleasure for me as I thought about you, the limitlessness of your mind and spirit, and how you might use this information to improve your life. I wish you every success in life and I hope that you create the life of your dreams.

BIBLIOGRAPHY

Chopra, Deepak. *Quantum Healing: Exploring the Frontiers of the Mind.* Bantam, 1990

Fezler, William D. *Creative Imagery-How to Visualize in all Five Senses.* Simon & Schuster, 1989

Fezler, William D. *Imagery for Healing, Knowledge & Power.* Fireside, 1990

Gawain, Shakti. *Creative Visualization.* New World Library, 2002

Lipton, Bruce. *The Biology of Belief.* Hay House, 2009

Robbins, Anthony. *Awaken the Giant Within.* Free Press, 1992

Ponder, Catherine. *Open Your Mind to Receive –New & Updated.* DeVorss & Co, 2007

Ponder, Catherine. *The Dynamic Laws of Prosperity.* Wilder Publications, 2009

Silva, Jose. *The Silva Mind Control Method* Pocket Books, 1991

Silva, Jose. *You the Healer: The World-Famous Silva Method on How to Heal Yourself and Others.* H.J.Kramer, 1991

Talbot, Michael. *The Holographic Universe.* Harper Perennial, 1992

Wolf, Fred Allen. *Taking the Quantum Leap.* Harper & Row, 1989

Printed in Great Britain
by Amazon.co.uk, Ltd.,
Marston Gate.